Portrait of Roger Bacon, O.F.M. *Doctor Mirabilis*
Holy Name College, Silver Spring, MD
Photo by F. Edward Coughlin, O.F.M.

KNOWLEDGE FOR LOVE:

FRANCISCAN SCIENCE
AS THE PURSUIT OF WISDOM

THE FRANCISCAN HERITAGE SERIES

General Editor
Joseph P. Chinnici, O.F.M.

Assistant Editor
Daria Mitchell, O.S.F.

Titles in the Franciscan Heritage Series

Knowledge for Love: Franciscan Science as the Pursuit of Wisdom
by Keith Douglass Warner, O.F.M.

*Women of the Streets: Early Franciscan Women
and Their Mendicant Vocation* by Darleen Pryds, Ph.D.

*Rejoicing in the Works of the Lord:
Beauty in the Franciscan Tradition* by Mary Beth Ingham, C.S.J.

Trinitarian Perspectives in the Franciscan Theological Tradition
by Maria Calisi

*The Franciscan Vision and the Gospel of John:
The San Damiano Crucifix, Francis and John, Creation and John*
by Michael D. Guinan, O.F.M.

*The Franciscan View of the Human Person:
Some Central Elements* by Dawn Nothwehr, O.S.F.

*A Franciscan View of Creation: Learning to Live
in a Sacramental World* by Ilia Delio, O.S.F.

*The Franciscan Intellectual Tradition: Tracing Its Origins and
Identifying Its Central Components* by Kenan Osborne, O.F.M.

KNOWLEDGE FOR LOVE:

FRANCISCAN SCIENCE
AS THE PURSUIT OF WISDOM

KEITH DOUGLASS WARNER, O.F.M.

VOLUME EIGHT
THE FRANCISCAN HERITAGE SERIES

Commission on the Franciscan Intellectual Tradition
of the English-speaking Conference
of the Order of Friars Minor
CFIT/ESC-OFM
2012

FRANCISCAN
INSTITUTE
PUBLICATIONS

St. Bonaventure University
St. Bonaventure, NY USA

© Franciscan Institute Publications
St. Bonaventure University
St. Bonaventure, NY 14778
2012

This booklet is the eighth in
The Franciscan Heritage Series
sponsored by the
Commission on the Franciscan Intellectual Tradition
of the English-speaking Conference of the
Order of Friars Minor
(CFIT/ESC-OFM)

General Editor
Joseph P. Chinnici, O.F.M.

Assistant Editor
Daria Mitchell, O.S.F.

ISBN13: 978-1-57659-361-5
ISBN10: 1-57659-361-4

Library of Congress Cataloging-in-Publication Data

Warner, Keith.
  Knowledge for love : Franciscan science as the pursuit of wisdom
/ Keith Douglass Warner.
        p. cm. -- (Franciscan heritage series / CFIT/ESC-OFM ; v. 8)
  Includes bibliographical references.
  ISBN 978-1-57659-361-5
  1. Franciscans. 2. Learning and scholarship. 3. Nature--Religious
aspects--Catholic Church. 4. Science--Study and teaching. I. Fran-
ciscan Institute (St. Bonaventure University) II. Title.
  BX360.W37 2012
  001.88'2713--dc23

                                                    2012022793

Printed and bound in the United States of America
BookMasters, Inc.
Ashland, Ohio

TABLE OF CONTENTS

DEDICATION

To Friar Finian McGinn, O.F.M.,
who taught so many of us
about the importance of culture, knowledge and love.

INTRODUCTION

On October 11, 1962 Pope John XXIII convened the Second Vatican Council, the most important event for the life of the Church in the modern age. This year we will celebrate the fiftieth anniversary of the Council which called for a renewal of spirit and a return to the charisms of the Church. In light of the Council's call for renewal, the Franciscan intellectual tradition was revived in late twentieth century, and the wealth of theology and philosophy that forms this tradition has been the source of scholarship in recent years. This Heritage Series of publications is intended to introduce the reader to the intellectual wealth of the tradition.

Among the many contributions Franciscans have made to the Church, perhaps the least known are the contributions of Franciscans to science. This may surprise many people, especially since Francis of Assisi considered himself a simple and unlettered man. However, his creation-centered spirituality had a profound influence on those who followed him. From the life of Francis we affirm the overflowing goodness of God. Creation is not on the fringe of divine power but flows out of the heart of an infinitely loving Creator. As a limited actualization of the divine self-diffusive good, creation is caught up in the mystery of the generation of the Word from the Father through the Spirit. It is a sacrament of God's loving presence and the first book of revelation. Francis embraced the material world as the place to find God. Rather than viewing the world from the top rung of the ladder of creation, he saw himself as part of creation. "He would call creatures, no matter how small by the name of 'brother' or 'sister,'" Bonaventure said, "because he knew they shared with him the same beginning."[1] Instead of using creatures to ascend to God (or using creatures for his own benefit), he found God in all creatures.

There are several important developments which influenced the rise of science in the Middle Ages. First, the *Sentences* of Peter Lombard introduced discussion of the world picture into academic theology which was considered the queen of sciences. Second, the translation of Aristotle's works into Latin by Boethius (sixth century) enabled scholars to apply Aristotelian logic to theological problems. The introduction of Aristotle's writings into the university curriculum coupled with the Arabic commentaries on these writings provided the foundation for the development of science in the High Middle Ages. Third, the translation of Plato's *Timaeus* into Latin and the availability of other classics, such as the works of Augustine, also helped forge the rise of science. The *Timaeus* became the central text for natural philosophy because it reconciled Platonic cosmogeny with the account of creation in Genesis. The cosmic order coupled with Aristotle's philosophy enabled scholars at the various universities – Oxford, Paris, Bologna – to debate cosmological questions. Creation was regarded as a book by which one could come to know God, and the task of the theologian was to help make the book of creation more legible. Hence medieval theologians were very interested in cosmology and entertained questions of the cosmos in the pursuit of theological truth.

Early Franciscan theologians such as Bonaventure and Scotus were attentive to the natural world as a source of theology. While Bonaventure's doctrine of exemplarism pointed to an integral relationship between God and creation, Scotus's doctrine of univocal being provided a theology of creation that resonates with modern science. Less known, however, are the Franciscans who followed Bonaventure and Scotus. In this small volume, Brother Keith Warner has provided an invaluable contribution by highlighting three Franciscan Friars who engaged the science of their day and developed scientific

---

[1] Bonaventure, *Legenda maior* 8:6, trans. Ewert H. Cousins, *Bonaventure: The Soul's Journey into God, the Tree of Life, The Major Life of Saint Francis* (New York: Paulist, 1978), 254-55.

insights along the lines of Franciscan spirituality. Perhaps the best known among these Friars is Roger Bacon, a disciple of Robert Grosseteste and the father of experimental science. He was influenced by the Islamic mathematician and philosopher Alhazen and developed a mathematical analysis of light and vision that eventually led to the understanding of optics. The other two Friars, Bartholomew the Englishman and Bernardino de Sahagún are less well known but their writings were extensive and significant.

This book comes at a time when the Church is grappling with complex developments in the sciences and their impact on culture. In his 1987 message to the Director of the Vatican Observatory Blessed Pope John Paul II stated that "science can purify religion from error and superstition; religion can purify science from idolatry and false absolutes. Each can draw the other into a wider world, a world in which both can flourish."[2] Speaking to the Papal Academy of Sciences, he said, "theologians and those working on the exegesis of Scripture need to be well informed regarding the results of the latest scientific research."[3] Commenting on the findings of various sciences, from molecular biology to paleontology, the Pope indicated that "the convergence in the results of these independent studies ... constitutes in itself a significant argument in favor of the theory (of evolution)." Openness to the modern sciences, according to John Paul, can help the Church remain on the path of truth and not wander off into error and superstition. More recently, the Pontifical Council of Culture has instituted a department dedicated to the dialogue between science and theology. Archbishop Gianfranco Ravasi, President of the Council, has described the importance of the Science and Religion dialogue for both Church and culture. Without a relationship between science

---

[2] Pope John Paul II, "Letter to Rev. George V. Coyne, S.J., Director of the Vatican Observatory," in Ted Peters (ed.), *Science and Theology: The New Consonance* (Boulder, CO: Westview Press, 1999), 157.

[3] Pope John Paul II, "Message to the Pontifical Academy of Sciences on Evolution," 3. http://www.ewtn.com/library/PAPALDOC/JP961022.HTM.

and faith, he indicates, scientific materialism can arise on
one hand and fideism or blind faith on the other. If religious
experience is to enter into dialogue with the world at large, it
must make use of concepts drawn from the culture around it
which includes modern science.

Although Brother Keith's book is an historical view of
Franciscans and science, it points to the fact that, since the
Middle Ages, Franciscans have been involved in the study of
nature. The relationship between Franciscans and science is
a "natural" one; creation is the place of God's dwelling. It is
the centrality of the Incarnation, however, that makes science more than just the study of nature. The integral relationship between creation and incarnation means that "we
discover ... in Jesus the divine clue as to the structure and
meaning not only of humanity but of the entire universe."[4]
The world is not a plurality of unrelated things but a true
unity, a *cosmos*, centered in Christ. As Zachary Hayes wrote,
"God creates toward an end. That end as embodied in Christ
points to a Christified world."[5] What may appear from the
sciences as a mechanical process is, on another level, a limit-
less mystery of productive love. "God's creative love freely
calls from within the world a created love that can freely re-
spond to God's creative call."[6] That created love is embodied
in Christ in whom all of creation finds its purpose. That is
why "a cosmos without Christ is a cosmos without a head ...
it simply does not hold together."[7] This universe is meaning-
ful and purposeful because it is grounded in Christ, the Word
of God.

Brother Keith extends this incarnational pillar to three
important areas of concern today: ecoliteracy, human dignity
and public health. He shows that Franciscans and science belong together; scientific knowledge can lead to wisdom when
it is filled with charity. Knowledge that deepens love orients

---

[4] Zachary Hayes, "Christ, Word of God and Exemplar of Humanity,"
Cord 46.1 (1996), 7.

[5] Zachary Hayes, *A Window to the Divine: a Study of Christian Cre-
ationTtheology* (Quincy, IL: Franciscan Press, 1997), 90.

[6] Hayes, *Window to the Divine,* 91.

[7] Hayes, "Christ, Word of God and Exemplar of Humanity," 13.

us to the world as brother and sister. We have much to offer this age of science because Franciscan spiritual values speak to a scientific age calling out for meaning and purpose; but we also have much to learn about ourselves. As we go forth in the spirit of Vatican II, I would encourage Franciscans to grow in scientific knowledge to enrich current and future explorations of our intellectual tradition.

Ilia Delio, O.S.F.
Woodstock Theological Center
Georgetown University

CHAPTER ONE

LOVE AND KNOWLEDGE
IN THE FRANCISCAN TRADITION

> Praised be You, my Lord, with all Your creatures, especially Sir Brother Sun, who is the day and through whom You give us light.
>
> Francis of Assisi, *The Canticle of the Creatures*[1]

Franciscans believe that creation is good. Francis loved creation, and gave thanks to God for it. *The Canticle of the Creatures* was the fruit of years of contemplative prayer in nature. As a troubadour, Francis praised God for creation, and praised creation for how it helped him to perceive God's presence in the material world. As a Franciscan scholar, Bonaventure articulated a theology of God as creator, and a philosophy to help us understand the world as God's creation. Bonaventure described creation as a book, and recommended we read it to better understand God.[2] This essay relates a

---

[1] Regis Armstrong, O.F.M. Cap., J.A. Wayne Hellmann, O.F.M. Conv., and William Short, O.F.M., eds., *Francis of Assisi: Early Documents, Volume I: The Saint* (New York: New City Press, 1999), 113.

[2] The metaphor of nature as a book for Christians to read was first proposed by Augustine. For a basic introduction to the Catholic tradition linking faith and reason, and how the Franciscan tradition builds upon this, see Zachary Hayes, O.F.M., *The Gift of Being: A Theology of Creation* (Collegeville: The Liturgical Press, 2001). "Book" is but one of more than a dozen metaphors Bonaventure used to communicate the theological significance of creation. See Zachary Hayes, O.F.M., "The Cosmos, a Symbol

few stories of how, in the Franciscan tradition, knowledge of creation can lead us to love of God.

Franciscan science is the knowledge of creation held by Franciscans, whether lay or vowed religious, women or men. In this definition, "science" means a broader way of knowing, a more holistic approach to knowledge of nature than typical of modern science. It refers back to the Latin *scientia*, meaning the broad sense of human knowledge of the world. Franciscan science has been lost, stolen or forgotten, but it could be retrieved. This essay argues we should recover an interest in the sciences to be faithful to our Catholic Franciscan tradition. There are many Franciscans who use science, although few fulfill the stereotypical image of a laboratory research scientist. If we understand science to mean this broader way of knowing nature, we can recognize many more Franciscans who use science in their work and ministry. Franciscan science always has a religious and moral purpose: to help us live loving, faith-filled lives in harmony with all of God's creation.

This essay extends the retrieval of the Franciscan intellectual tradition into the sciences. Retrieving Franciscan philosophy and theology is vitally important, but Franciscan science bears wisdom, too, for it can help us live as creatures of God in right relationship with creation. Franciscans taught and researched science for much the same reason as any Franciscan pursued intellectual work: to grow in love, service and wisdom. Retrieving Franciscan science is necessary to capture the full breadth of the Franciscan tradition.

Modern science is a very powerful way of knowing, and many people today believe it is the ultimate source of truth. Science has a powerful set of tools to describe the world, but on its own, science cannot tell human beings how to live a good life. Scientific skills are essential to live in our technological age, but society today seems to place so much importance on science that we are neglecting other dimensions of our humanity. As a human family, our scientific and technical

of the Divine," in *Franciscan Theology of the Environment: An Introductory Reader*, ed. Dawn M. Nothwehr, O.S.F. (Quincy, IL: Franciscan Press, 2002).

skills have grown immensely. We have not, however, grown in wisdom, or the capacity to make good choices. Some students today describe their education as pulling them in contradictory directions, as fostering a fragmented learning experience. This essay relates three examples of Franciscan friars who engaged the science of their era, and who integrated their intellectual skills into their identity as Franciscans.

Friar Bartholomew the Englishman (c. 1203–1272) taught his fellow Franciscans with the best available scientific knowledge to prepare them for preaching in foreign lands among unfamiliar peoples. Bartholomew left his position at the University of Paris to help establish the Franciscan Order in Germany, on the frontier of Christian Europe. He taught countless young friars preparing for ministry, and from his classroom teaching he created a program of studies, akin to a curriculum guide or teacher's manual. Organized in the format of a medieval encyclopedia, *On the Properties of Things* circulated far beyond Franciscan schools to become one of the most influential sources of information of this era. Bartholomew is an example of a brilliant Franciscan teacher using knowledge of nature to help his students, and through his famous book, countless others.

Friar Roger Bacon (c. 1220–1294) conducted research into the natural world to advance scientific knowledge in service of the Church. As a leader in the Medieval Oxford Franciscan School, he was the friar who made the greatest contribution to the development of modern science. Roger studied light and vision, used mathematics and maps to describe the earth, and insisted that direct observation is essential to accurate knowledge of nature. He outlined the conceptual foundation upon which the modern scientific experimental method was built. Roger is an example of a Franciscan scientist who understood his research activities to have religious meaning.

Friar Bernardino de Sahagún (1499-1590) investigated the life, worldview and culture of indigenous peoples in New Spain (now Mexico) to interpret these for his fellow Franciscans. He sailed across the Atlantic Ocean to become a missionary and spent five decades studying and documenting nature and culture in Mesoamerica. He is best known for creating a report with some 2,000 illustrations on the cultural and natural history of New Spain. *La Historia General de las Cosas de Nueva Espana* (*The General History of the Things of New Spain*), commonly referred to as *The Florentine Codex*, is one of the most significant documents in the history of contact between human cultures. Bernardino is considered the first anthropologist, anticipating many of the methodologies used in anthropology today. He was particularly interested in Aztec concepts of health and medicine. He is an example of a Franciscan who used his intellectual gifts in service of the friars' project of global evangelization.

The Franciscan tradition is a practical wisdom tradition, meaning that learning is for the sake of furthering our love of God and love of the good.[3] Franciscan science always has a purpose beyond that of the acquisition of knowledge for one's self. Francis believed that selfish motivations for learning are spiritually dangerous, and insisted that the pursuit of knowledge always be in service of God and neighbor.[4] Learning always has some kind of moral implication, in other words, ethical responsibility for the one who grows in knowledge. In the Franciscan tradition, learning should contribute to our wisdom, to making good choices, in order to live a good life and love God with greater passion. Wisdom requires integrating love and knowledge in order to live a life of faith. Thus, Franciscan science is for love.

The balance of this chapter will introduce critical contemporary perspectives on science. Chapters two, three and four present the lives of Franciscan friars who used science and scientific ways of knowing in their service of the Gospel.[5] Each of these three chapters will provide a

[3] Zachary Hayes, "Franciscan Tradition as Wisdom Tradition," *Spirit and Life: A Journal of Contemporary Franciscanism* 7 (1997), 27-40.

[4] See Admonition VII, in Armstrong, Hellman, and Short, eds., *Francis of Assisi: Early Documents, Volume I: The Saint*, 132.

[5] A note about the methods used in this essay is in order. Three individuals are used as case studies not because they are representative Franciscan friars (they are not), but rather because they are the best examples from the Franciscan tradition of the contemporary themes this essay presents. The historical data in this essay is derived entirely from

biographical sketch of the friar, introduce his major work, provide examples of his scientific activity, and propose some contemporary implications of their life and work. The concluding chapter reviews cross-cutting implications from these examples, and proposes what it might mean to retrieve the Franciscan tradition of science today. The concluding chapter reviews cross-cutting implications from these examples, proposes what it might mean to retrieve the Franciscan tradition of science.

INVESTIGATING SCIENCE IN ACTION

The most basic definition of science is but two words: justified knowledge. This indicates that having scientific knowledge is different than holding an opinion or a belief. It also suggests that people need to agree upon the method of justifying that knowledge. Debates about what constitutes sufficient method for justification go back thousands of years. The branch of philosophy that grapples with this question is epistemology.

The origins of science can be traced back to the Ancient Greeks, and specifically to Aristotle. He combined observation of the natural world with logical reasoning about universal principles. He classified biological organisms by their traits. He described patterns of difference and change over time, and their causes. He developed techniques of careful observation of the natural world. For example, he examined chick embryos by breaking open one egg every day to observe its progressive development. He developed the

---

the research of specialists (history, philosophy, literature, anthropology) who have studied these men, their works, and their era. Quotes from these friars themselves are taken from the English-language secondary sources written by modern specialist scholars.

Since scholarship during the Middle Ages was essentially restricted to males, the available examples for this study are only men. For a discussion of obstacles to women conducting Franciscan theology see Margaret Carney, O.S.F., "The Feminine Side of Franciscan Theology," in *The History of Franciscan Theology*, ed. Kenan B. Osborne, O.F.M. (St. Bonaventure, NY: The Franciscan Institute, 1994; reprinted in 2007).

principle of justified knowledge. In Ancient Greece this type of intellectual activity was conducted in the field of natural philosophy, and Aristotle's writings about the natural world were the most influential prior to the scientific revolution in the seventeenth century.[6]

Much of Aristotle's work was lost to Europe after the collapse of the Roman Empire, but was rediscovered – or retrieved – starting in the 1100s. His key writings in natural philosophy were retrieved by medieval scholars who blended his insights into contemporary ways of understanding nature. Across the thousand years of medieval Europe, natural philosophy and its speculation about the religious significance of nature evolved toward focused, systematic observation of actual phenomena and mathematical measurements of nature. Thus, the broader field of natural philosophy gave way to medieval science, or knowledge of nature using the tools of that era.[7] Bartholomew, Roger and Bernardino were medieval scientists and thus profoundly influenced by the Bible, Church teachings, Aristotle, and contemporary cultural values. As important intellectual figures, they also actively contributed to shaping its developmental trajectory.

Medieval science can be understood as an intermediate stage between Aristotle's Greek natural philosophy and the European scientific revolution of the seventeenth century. The leading figures in the European scientific revolution, such as Galileo, Isaac Newton, and Renee Descartes, built upon the foundations laid by medieval science.[8] Modern science is distinguished from earlier forms of science chiefly by its method of determining justified knowledge. Over time, scientists developed a method for justifying knowledge that tested a hypothesis, commonly known as the scientific

---

[6] Edward Grant, *A History of Natural Philosophy: From the Ancient World to the Nineteenth Century* (Cambridge: Cambridge University Press, 2007).

[7] The simplified definitions in this section will be discussed throughout this book, drawing extensively from Edward Grant, *The Foundations of Modern Science in the Middle Ages: Their Religious, Institutional, and Intellectual Contexts* (Cambridge: Cambridge University Press, 1996).

[8] Samir Okasha, *Philosophy of Science: A Very Short Introduction* (London: Oxford University Press, 2002).

method. This method builds upon prior knowledge to propose a hypothesis which can be evaluated, one that can potentially be proven false. This hypothesis is tested with evidence, and then a deduction can be made. This basic approach of deploying the scientific method is applied today in more sophisticated ways by scientists.

One of the most important books in the history and philosophy of science, *The Structure of Scientific Revolutions*, was written by Thomas Kuhn.[9] Most prior explanations of the history of science presented science as a rational, objective, and value-free pursuit of scientific facts. Most historians had presented these facts as though they existed independently in nature, awaiting human discovery, akin to buried treasure. Kuhn showed how human beings actually conducted science – in other words, how scientific knowledge is actually created – rather than how scientists and scientific knowledge are represented in idealized stories. Nature exists independently of humans, but scientific knowledge is created by people, using certain methods to justify their knowledge. Science is a human practice, the product of human work, and subject to the many influences (both rational and irrational) of any social activity. Kuhn showed that scientists are deeply influenced by social values, and some behave in irrational ways. He described how scientific discovery has been impeded by scientists refusing to accept new data and new ways of understanding the world.

In describing what science is and how it evolves, Kuhn presented a major concept for this essay: paradigm. Knowledge exists in human beings who organize it into a mental model, or paradigm. Kuhn argued that all knowledge, including scientific knowledge, is more than a list of data or facts. He argued that a paradigm consists of knowledge, but also of shared assumptions about how the world operates. Thus, a paradigm consists of a relatively stable view of nature and society, shaped by data, knowledge, values and beliefs.

---

[9] Thomas Kuhn, *The Structure of Scientific Revolutions* (Chicago: University of Chicago Press, 1962).

Kuhn demonstrated that paradigms are resistant to change, and that scientists, like most human beings, are reluctant to abandon old paradigms and to embrace new ones. He argued that scientific development is not linear, but rather, it is relatively stable with sudden periods of rapid change. This is what he meant by "scientific revolutions," which he also described as a "paradigm shift." A scientific paradigm persists in a relatively stable equilibrium, but is occasionally disrupted, and then undergoes a rapid reconfiguration. Kuhn made the controversial claim that the overall direction of scientific progress is not always built upon prior knowledge, and does not necessarily progress toward greater truth. As justification, he showed how Einstein's theory of relativity shares, in some respects, more with Aristotle's theories of twenty-five centuries prior than with the ideas of Newton, just three centuries prior.[10]

Subsequent scholars built upon Kuhn's ideas about paradigms by more explicitly incorporating people, and they developed the concept of a "knowledge system."[11] A knowledge system is a network of people, their social values and assumptions, and the knowledge they share. Thus, by studying a knowledge system, one can understand the network of what is known and by whom. This approach asserts that knowledge does not exist apart from human "knowers" who investigate, gather, organize, interpret and selectively represent it. If one accepts Kuhn's argument that science is created by scientists in a social activity, one must also accept the fact that social values can readily influence science, even though this fact is frequently disregarded in popular accounts of science and scientists. Using a knowledge system approach, anthropologists have described how indigenous peoples have developed their own forms of "Indigenous Ecological Knowledge," which

---

[10] Okasha, *Philosophy of Science: A Very Short Introduction.*

[11] Many scholars now describe knowledge systems, but for an introduction see Niels Röling, "The Emergence of Knowledge Systems Thinking: A Changing Perception of Relationships among Innovation, Knowledge Process and Configuration," *Knowledge and Policy: The International Journal of Knowledge Transfer* 5, no. 1 (1992): 42-64.

can be evaluated in much the same way as modern, Western science.[12]

The most radical question raised by Kuhn's work was: Does science exist apart from human beings? His conclusion was no, it is the product of human activity, and therefore requires human beings to create it. To describe some knowledge as "science" requires human beings to gather evidence, analyze and synthesize this, and then justify their knowledge with certain methods. Scientific "facts" and "truths" do not exist hidden in nature, awaiting human "discovery." Nature exists, and reality exists, and these can be experienced through the senses. Science is a means of assembling data to construct and organize knowledge, but it depends upon human actions, and thus it is shaped, in part, by social values.

This essay investigates Bernardino, Bartholomew and Roger Bacon as medieval scientists in action. We would be disappointed were we to ask "What did they learn about nature and culture from their scientific study that I can find useful for my life today?" Virtually none of their data is directly relevant to scientific knowledge or theories or methodologies used by scientists today. Yet we should not expect it to be so, given the many scientific revolutions that have taken place over the past five centuries.

A more helpful question to bring to this essay would be: "Why did these Franciscans investigate nature and society, and how did their scientific work fit within their vocation to live and preach the Gospel as Franciscans?" This line of inquiry opens up the possibility of reflecting upon the relationship of love and knowledge in our own lives. All three made significant contributions to the human understanding of the natural world and its goodness, and they provide an example of a Franciscan approach to knowing and loving the world. Thus, this essay does not provide instruction in how to conduct science, but rather, suggests how those inspired by Francis of Assisi today can incorporate scientific knowledge

---

[12] For an introduction see Keith Douglass Warner, O.F.M., "Teaching Environmental Scientists from Country: Integral Wisdom for a New Australia," *Learning Communities: International Journal of Learning in Social Contexts* 2, 1 (2010): 102-14.

into living the Gospel in the twenty-first century. The conclusion will outline what Franciscan science might look like
today, specifically in the fields of the environment, culture,
and human health.

CHAPTER TWO

BARTHOLOMEW THE ENGLISHMAN,
AND HIS BOOK FOR PILGRIMS

(We) put our hand to the properties of the sensible world ... that we may elicit from the properties of things matter for divine praise, and the working of the Creator. For the unseen things of God are clearly seen, being understood by the things that are made, as the Apostle says. And thus we intend to introduce into this little work, as into a compendium, the properties of any thing of this world or of its contents, so that through the similitude of corporeal properties, we may be able more easily to understand the spiritual and mystical meaning in the Holy Scriptures.

Bartholomew the Englishman,
On the Properties of Things[13]

Francis wanted his brothers to be pilgrims and strangers.[14] Franciscan itinerancy, or religiously inspired movement through the world as an expression of living the Gospel, is

---

[13] Found in book 8 of *De proprietatibus rerum*, taken from Roger French and Andrew Cunningham, *Before Science: The Invention of the Friars' Natural Philosophy* (London: Scolar Press, 1996), 210.

[14] The term "pilgrims and strangers" is derived from 1 Peter 2:11 and is found in the writings of Francis: *The Rule* chapter 6, *Testament* 24, in Armstrong, Hellmann, and Short, eds., *Francis of Assisi: Early Documents, Volume I: The Saint*.

a response to the humility of Jesus Christ.[15] Francis understood Jesus to have been a traveler, from the right hand of
God to and across the Earth, and back to heaven. To imitate
the poverty and vulnerability of Jesus, friars were to live
without the resources, stability, and protection of monastic
enclosure. They were to journey through the world.

The Franciscan movement developed during the period
of medieval history in which people began to move about
Europe. In twelfth century art, images of travelers appear:
pilgrims, merchants, traders, wayfarers, crusaders, walkers,
mariners and rowers.[16] This suggests that paradigm shift
in human understanding of nature was underway. In the
early middle ages, nature had been depicted with mythical
creatures, but this gave way to more accurate renditions of
plants, animals, and landscapes, reflecting careful human
observation.[17] The shift from monks in monasteries to friars
on the road was but one expression of broad changes taking
place in medieval society. For some critics, including some
Church authorities, the travels of Franciscans were seen as
a suspicious form of religious life.[18]

Francis commissioned his brothers to travel through the
world preaching the Gospel. He could not have anticipated
all the people, places and things they would encounter. In
the 1210s, with small groups of men, this could be done simply, without an organized program. In just a few short years,
however, the brotherhood grew exponentially, from dozens to
more than five thousand. It was transformed into a large,
diverse and dispersed religious order. The leadership of the

---

[15] Keith Douglass Warner, O.F.M., "Pilgrims and Strangers: The
Evangelical Spirituality of Itinerancy of the Early Franciscan Friars,"
Spirit and Life: A Journal of Contemporary Franciscanism 10 (2000), 63-
170.

[16] Elizabeth Keen, *The Journey of a Book: Bartholomew the Englishman
and the Properties of Things* (Canberra: ANU E-press, 2007), 57.

[17] Marie-Dominique Chenu, O.P., *Nature, Man, and Society in the
Twelfth Century: Essays on New Theological Perspectives in the Latin
West*, trans. Jerome Taylor and Lester K. Little (Chicago: The University
of Chicago Press, 1968).

[18] Keen, *The Journey of a Book: Bartholomew the Englishman and the
Properties of Things*.

Catholic Church embraced this movement, but insisted the Order prepare, scrutinize and approve its new members before allowing them to preach formal sermons. This period witnessed the rise of diverse expressions of religious fervor, from groups seeking to renew the Church according to its primitive spirit (such as the Franciscans), to groups that rejected core Christian beliefs, such as the Cathars. This breakaway group believed that only the spiritual realm was pure and that the material world was evil.

Friar Jordan of Giano related the story of the first Franciscan mission to what is now Germany. The friars sent were unable to speak the German language, however they heard the word "ya," and discovered that when they used it, good things happened. However, when asked – in German – if they were themselves Cathars, they answered "ya" and suffered physical punishment by the authorities.[19] For the friars to faithfully go through the entire world preaching the Gospel, their message would have to be intelligible. They would have to understand the world and its diverse cultures if they were to avoid confusion and conflicts. The Franciscans were going to need a program of education to fulfill their vocation. This would certainly include languages, theology and philosophy, but also science and culture.[20]

Friar Bartholomew the Englishman addressed this need. He was trained in Scripture, joined the Franciscans at the University of Paris during Francis's lifetime, and became an instructor of young friars in Germany within five years of Francis's death. Bartholomew wrote his book, *On the Properties of Things*, to introduce the world to young Franciscans. It was so useful that it was adopted by many other teachers in other schools across Europe, and subsequently became a reference manual for preachers. He presented basic ideas about God, the universe, culture, nature and the Earth as

---

[19] Jordan of Giano, "Chronicle of Jordan of Giano," in *Early Franciscan Classics*, ed. David Temple, O.F.M. (Oakland: Franciscan Fathers of the St. Barbara Province, 1954), Paragraph 5, 140.

[20] Bert Roest, *A History of Franciscan Education (c. 1210-1517)* (Leiden: Brill, 2000).

these were understood at this time. It became one of the most influential books in the late middle ages.[21]

Bartholomew wrote *On the Properties of Things* as an instructor's manual, or a kind of comprehensive syllabus. Bartholomew had several goals in mind: to provide basic keywords and ideas to prepare the friars to study philosophy and theology; to prepare them to preach to ordinary people who worked the land; and to help them understand the religious meaning of creation.

On the Properties of Things is valuable to us today because it conveys how an early friar taught his students to understand nature. It does not present modern scientific information, but rather a Franciscan attitude toward knowledge of nature. Bartholomew's book sought to persuade the reader that earthly things can lead us to an understanding of heavenly things, and to reconciliation with God.[22] Bartholomew introduced basic keywords and information about nature which would help a student understand the metaphorical religious significance of creation in Bonaventure's spiritual classic, *The Soul's Journey into God*.[23] Bonaventure is an important theologian in the Franciscan tradition, and conveyed through *The Soul's Journey into God* his vision of an idealized religious journey through life, of how creation can lead us to mystical union with God. Bartholomew's book provided the practical knowledge of nature that medieval people would need to undertake the religious journey recommended by Bonaventure. Francis, Bonaventure and Bartholomew believed that knowledge is for love. All three asserted, in their own way, that the knowledge of nature has a religious purpose, and can help us grow in love.

This chapter begins with an outline of Bartholomew's Franciscan vocation, followed by an introduction to *On the*

---

[21] Keen, *The Journey of a Book: Bartholomew the Englishman and the Properties of Things*.

[22] Keen, *The Journey of a Book*.

[23] Ewert Cousins, *Bonaventure: The Soul's Journey into God, The Tree of Life, The Life of St. Francis*, The Classics of Western Spirituality (New York: Paulist Press, 1978). See especially the introduction for the influence of Francis on Bonaventure.

Properties of Things, its content, organization and purpose. This is followed by an explanation of how Bartholomew's book reflects medieval scientific knowledge. It concludes with some contemporary implications of Bartholomew as a Franciscan medieval scientist.

BARTHOLOMEW'S FRANCISCAN VOCATION

The historical record of Bartholomew is thin. Historians can only describe with confidence that he became a Franciscan friar; taught the Bible at the Franciscan house of studies in Paris in the late 1220s; was commissioned in 1231 to teach the friars at Magdeburg (not far from present-day Berlin in Germany); and was elected a Provincial Minister (regional leader of the Franciscans). Circumstantial evidence suggests some additional details, but these are necessarily speculative.[24]

Bartholomew was called "the Englishman," so it is reasonable to presume he was born in England. We know nothing about his educational background, but he would have needed advanced training to be qualified as a teacher of scripture at the University of Paris. He was likely born between 1200 and 1203. If he studied at the University of Oxford, it might have been in the years between 1214 and 1220, and he probably would have met Robert Grosseteste (described in the next chapter). If he had been teaching at the University of Paris prior to joining the Franciscans, he might have arrived around 1220, and entered the Franciscans in roughly 1225.

Jordan of Giano identified 1231 as the year Bartholomew was assigned to teach at Magdeburg.[25] Analysis of what was and was not included in his book suggests that Bartholomew completed it around 1245. Some evidence suggests Bartholomew became the Provincial Minister of Austria in 1247,

---

[24] Seymour outlines Bartholomew's biography on pages 1-14. He cites others who believe Bartholomew was elected provincial in more than one province. See M. C. Seymour, *Bartolomaeus Anglicus and His Encyclopedia* (Aldershot, UK: Variorum, 1992).

[25] Jordan of Giano, "Chronicle of Jordan of Giano." Paragraph 60, 156.

and in 1255, Bohemia (in what is now the Czech Republic), and Saxony (around Magdeburg) in 1262. He apparently died as Provincial Minister of Saxony in 1272. He might have participated in the General Chapter of 1257 (the international legislative body that guides the Franciscan Order), at which Bonaventure was appointed Minister General of the Franciscans. An archive has a document that purports to be a letter from Bonaventure to Bartholomew in 1266, although this is questionable.[26]

Bartholomew was a teacher, and participated in medieval university life. Bartholomew taught Scripture at Paris, and this included explaining the world of the Bible, its people, plants, and places.[27] Thus, he made the Scriptures accessible to young friars far from the prestige of Paris. The University of Paris was the most sophisticated educational institution of this era. Universities were relatively new, and they only began to take shape during the lifetime of Francis. Previously, monasteries had the only schools. Classes were informal, and intended to help monks learn about scripture, liturgy, history and prayer. Few books were available for use, and since they had to be crafted by hand, they were extremely valuable. Study in monasteries had existed to foster piety and devotion, and not intellectual development leading to a degree or skills for a profession.

"The cathedral schools" of the eleventh and twelfth centuries were urban versions of the monastery schools that provided more practical training and skills. As European society became more urbanized, cathedral schools adapted the monastic educational program to prepare priests, especially in reading the Bible. The universities subsequently evolved from the cathedral schools. The instructors and "classrooms" moved out of the cathedral and into private houses, often of

---

[26] Seymour, *Bartolomaeus Anglicus and His Encyclopedia*, 11.

[27] Medieval scholars generally assumed that the Bible contained all necessary knowledge about the world, but that the fall of Adam and expulsion from the Garden of Eden meant that sin clouded human understanding. In addition to its literal meaning, the Bible had allegorical or religious meanings, and the early Church Fathers, or Patristic writers, articulated these. See French and Cunningham, *Before Science: The Invention of the Friars' Natural Philosophy*.

parish priests. The priest-teachers offered their ground floor as a classroom, and the students usually lived in these houses.

Students would typically begin at university around the age of fifteen. They would study the seven "liberal arts," which defined the Bachelor of Arts degree at the medieval university.[28] A liberal arts education was composed of seven subjects, organized into two groups: three language subjects, and four numerical subjects. The three language subjects were studied first: grammar – or how to read and write; rhetoric – or public persuasion; and dialectic – or the study of logic and argument.[29] These were followed by the four subjects of the physical world using numbers: arithmetic, geometry, astronomy, and music.[30] This was the standard program of study for any educated person at this time (which was only a tiny minority of men, less than five percent). After completing the liberal arts, one received a bachelor's degree and was eligible to pursue an advanced degree, such as the Master of Theology. This was the intellectual world that the friars encountered at the universities of Paris and Oxford.[31]

Franciscan religious life and medieval universities began at roughly the same time, and they both grew in importance to impact Western Europe throughout the thirteenth century and beyond. The rise of universities reflected a profound shift in how medieval Europe viewed the natural world and the importance of knowledge. Historians describe twelfth-century European society as rediscovering nature, the cosmos, its reality and religious meaning.[32] At the beginning of the twelfth century, monastic and cathedral schools perceived nature as a religious idea, as a metaphor for the idea of creation. The rise of universities took a different approach to

---

[28] These were distinct from "the servile arts" or skills needed for manual labor. The seven liberal arts were for the "freeman" (*liber*), not the slave or servant.

[29] These three were known as the *trivium*.

[30] These four were known as the *quadrivium*.

[31] James Cato, ed., *The History of the University of Oxford* (Oxford: Clarendon Press, 1984).

[32] Chenu, *Nature, Man, and Society in the Twelfth Century: Essays on New Theological Perspectives in the Latin West.*

knowledge that reflected renewed human curiosity about nature and the universe, and about the relationship between God and creation. Nature was still understood to be religious in character, but men investigated it as a material reality in and of itself. Scholars were no longer satisfied with merely proclaiming the religious reality of the universe, but set out to explain nature's workings as a way of understanding God's work in the world (knowledge, or *scientia*). The Bible and theology were still very important subjects; to these were added the study of the universe and of nature. The investigation of nature dramatically expanded the scope of knowledge during this period

The Franciscan friars and the universities mutually influenced each other.[33] The friars went to university towns, studied, recruited teachers to teach and then to join. They taught all kinds of students in their study houses, including their own young members. Many men joined Franciscan life to participate in the intellectual life of Church and society. Friars debated with their intellectual peers, and they made important contributions to the fields of philosophy and theology in the late middle ages. Study and learning were integral to living the Gospel as Franciscans.[34]

Bartholomew's Franciscan vocation is all the more remarkable in this context. He joined the Franciscans at the elite University of Paris, but within a few years was sent to the unruly frontier of Christian Europe. Compared to Paris, Magdeburg was a backwater. There were no universities in Germany, so Bartholomew would have had to bring all his own teaching supplies from Paris, perhaps on a mule. He helped establish Franciscan life by teaching young men about the world into which they would be sent.

---

[33] Franciscan and Dominican friars actively shaped university curriculum during the middle ages. See French and Cunningham, *Before Science: The Invention of the Friars' Natural Philosophy*..

[34] Roest, *A History of Franciscan Education (c. 1210-1517)*.

THE WORLD ACCORDING TO BARTHOLOMEW'S BOOK

The Latin title of *On the Properties of Things* could also be informally translated: "The Characteristics of Material Stuff."[35] It was translated into medieval English and French in the fourteenth century, and in the fifteenth century into Spanish, Dutch, and Italian.[36] With the creation of the mechanical printing press, eleven editions of the book were published between 1472 and 1492.[37] That this work was repeatedly copied, translated and printed over these centuries demonstrates its evident popularity and usefulness. However, it was cast aside during the scientific revolution.

Bartholomew describes the purpose of his book as helping the reader to understand the Bible and creation, and their symbolic religious meaning. He asserts that understanding the characteristics of the created world will help a person pray, for it is the properties of things that one first experiences wonder.[38] The book has nineteen sections with three overarching themes: God and angels; human beings and society; and the universe and the natural world.

Bartholomew did not present his own original research, but rather synthesized and organized the knowledge system of his time. The Bible was his most important source,

---

[35] Keen, *The Journey of a Book: Bartholomew the Englishman and the Properties of Things*; Juris G. Lidaka, "Bartholomaeus Anglicus in the Thirteenth Century," in *Pre-Modern Encyclopaedic Texts – Proceedings of the Second Comers Congress, Groningen, 1-4 July 1996*, ed. Peter Binkley (Leiden: Brill, 1997).

[36] Gerald E. Se Boyar, O.F.M., "Bartolomeus and His Encyclopedia," *The Journal of English and Germanic Philology* XIX (1920). For more information about mss., see Seymour, *Bartolomaeus Anglicus and His Encyclopedia*. Seymour lists 165 handwritten full or partial manuscripts. The manuscript consists of about 400 folios which we today would describe as 800 pages. No copies remain from Bartholomew's lifetime. There is no definitive Latin version, and thus no modern English translation.

[37] Keen, *The Journey of a Book: Bartholomew the Englishman and the Properties of Things*. Setting up a printing press to publish a book of this size represented an enormous investment of resources.

[38] French and Cunningham, *Before Science: The Invention of the Friars' Natural Philosophy*, 215.

followed by Aristotle.[39] During the twelfth century, Europe
"rediscovered" Aristotle's writings, and their impact on medieval thinking cannot be overstated.[40] The translation of Aristotle's works into Latin revolutionized medieval Western
European thinking about nature, for they challenged the as-
sumption that the Bible contained all knowledge. Aristotle's
works undermined the early medieval scientific paradigm,
much as Darwin's explanation of evolution revolutionized
our understanding of life on Earth. Aristotle's approach was
attractive to medieval scholars because it was more practical
and accurate than the existing paradigm, which emphasized
a symbolic interpretation of nature. Most scholars and theologians embraced Aristotle's paradigm, and medieval universities provided the arena in which this knowledge could be
taught, studied, and further developed.

Bartholomew presented the Aristotelian paradigm. His
presentation of knowledge follows the approach to the organization of knowledge common to that era.[41] Its structure
conveys a medieval religious vision of the purpose of knowledge. Bartholomew presented the natural world as a source
of both wonder and praise,[42] blending together its earthiness
and its moral significance.[43] Thus, he draws on Aristotle's ap-

---

[39] Bartholomew drew from eighty-eight authoritative classical authors,
and cited 161 different sources of material. The number and organization
of cross-references suggests that he proceeded first in note form. See
Seymour, *Bartolomaeus Anglicus and His Encyclopedia*.

[40] Aristotle's works were lost to Western Europe with the breakup of
the Roman Empire, but were copied and studied across the Arab world,
from present-day Spain to Iraq. It is likely that the writings attributed
to Aristotle were produced by a community of scholars, much as *On the
Properties of Things* reflects the community of students gathered around
Bartholomew. See Grant, *A History of Natural Philosophy: From the
Ancient World to the Nineteenth Century*, 28-33.

[41] Bartholomew does not take up any of the controversial elements
of Aristotle's work. His purpose appears to be to record and present,
and not to argue or speculate. Seymour, *Bartolomaeus Anglicus and His
Encyclopedia*.

[42] D.C. Greetham, "The Concept of Nature in Bartolomaeus Anglicus,"
Journal of the History of Ideas 41, no. 4 (1980): 663-77.

[43] For example, metaphors of fertility or agricultural fecundity were
useful for explaining the life of the friars. There was a well-traveled path
"... for scholars, whether mendicant or monastic, to use imagery of the

proach to explain the components and structure of nature, and he incorporates this into his Catholic worldview. In this sense, he merely continues the Catholic tradition of faith and reason.[44]

---

vine, the beehive, the seed, the gleaner, the cultivation of fertile ground and of female fertility to denote the active work of spreading God's word, nurturing Christian souls and obtaining the rewards of salvation." Keen, *The Journey of a Book: Bartholomew the Englishman and the Properties of Things*, 31-35.

[44] Hayes, *The Gift of Being: A Theology of Creation*.

THE 19 SECTIONS ON THE PROPERTIES OF THINGS

1. On God and the names of God – Provides a standard medieval understanding of God, drawn from early patristic and contemporary authorities.

2. On the traits of angels – Describes angels in general, their nature, their intellect, and appearance in form; explains the fall of evil angels, and their powers of temptation.

3. On the soul and reason – Presents the human person, soul, body and sense, and spirit.

4. On the bodily humors – Describes the four elements and their related humors which compose the human body.

5. On the parts of the body – Surveys the parts of the human body, the limbs, and the complex organs, and proceeds to a lengthy description of its exact configuration and activity. Most chapters describe the ailments to which the organ is subject, usually in a list of potentially morbid symptoms or conditions.

6. On daily life – Describes the attributes naturally inherent to human life (such as Biblical categories of man and woman), and the external activities, such as food and drink, sleep and wakefulness, labor and rest. Prescribes hygiene through moderation.

7. On diseases and poisons – Presents an account of individual diseases and their causes. Each chapter begins with a description of diseases that afflict parts of the body, following the medieval ordering from head to foot, and goes on to describe the symptoms and progress of the disease, and then concludes by specifying treatment and medicines. Concludes with a summary of medicines and the duties of doctors.

8. On earth and the heavenly bodies – Presents the world and the heavens: the spheres and circles of heavens; the zodiac; the motions of the planets; the sun and moon; comets and fixed stars; and the theory of light.

9. On time and motion – Provides a description of the major divisions of the year.

10. On matter, form and fire – Presents a general introduction to matter and form and the elements which together

provide the underlying metaphysical basis of the rest of the book.

11. On the air and weather – Provides information on the air, with concern about its impact on human health.

12. On birds – Presents the inhabitants of the air, including four insects (bee, gnat, cicada, locust) and the bat.

13. On water and fishes – Proceeds to the nature of water and wells, standing pools, rivers and streams, lakes, individual rivers, the sea, bodies of water mentioned in the Bible, and fish.

14. On the earth and its surface – Provides a general description of the world and mountains, with a detailed gazetteer of mountains in the Bible.

15. On regions and places – This provides the most extensive index of places of any medieval book. Describes Europe and former Roman provinces of North Africa and Asia Minor and Bible lands, providing information on locations, inhabitants, cities, states, soils, woods, rivers and lakes.

16. On rocks, gems and minerals – Introduces basic minerals and elements in the earth.

17. On plants and trees – Presents 195 chapters about plants, which is the longest section.

18. On land animals – Describes various forms of animals that do not fly or swim.

19. On colors, smells and tastes, substances, measurements, numbers and music – Describes natural phenomena apprehended by the five senses: colors, taste, numbers, weights and music.

On the Properties of Things emerged from Bartholomew's teaching. The style is like that of an educated teacher toward pupils, providing tools to help students visualize and memorize the content. Drawing from the most authoritative scholars of this era, he "read" or lectured on the essential knowledge that a student friar would need to know.[45] Handwritten books in this era were very expensive, and libraries were rare. Students usually took notes from their morning lecture on writing tablets made of wax or wood, and then later in the day they would commit these notes to memory. The tablet would be wiped clean for use in class the next day. Bartholomew lectured, and perhaps a few very good students would have memorized and later transcribed entire lectures. Bartholomew was the author of this work, but his students may have helped with early drafts. Bartholomew created his book in a Franciscan study house, and it had practical use for its original Franciscan audience.

On the Properties of Things presents information within a typical thirteenth century knowledge system: first God, followed by angels, man, the Earth and sky, and finally, other expressions of nature. Several examples illustrate how this material was presented. Book 8 presents information on the material world, drawing from Greek and early Christian philosophers. Bartholomew presents the constellations of the zodiac and the other planets as existing in a belt that rotates around the Earth. Medieval scholars considered the sun and moon to be planets, but worthy of special attention due to their role in the Genesis creation account. Medieval astronomers struggled to explain why the planets moved the way they did, and Bartholomew skipped over this problem. This section closes with a description of the physics of light, which was considered a physical substance and essential part of creation.

---

[45] Keen, *The Journey of a Book: Bartholomew the Englishman and the Properties of Things*. He drew from eighty-eight authoritative classical authors, and cited 161 different sources of material. The number and organization of cross-references suggests that he proceeded first in note form. See Seymour, *Bartolomaeus Anglicus and His Encyclopedia*.

Books 14 and 15 provide detailed information on geographic features found in the Holy Land, the Mediterranean region, and what we would call Western Europe. Book 14 is primarily about mountains, especially those referenced in the Bible. The most important contribution of book 15 is its gazetteer, or dictionary of places, which was the most extensive yet to appear in the Middle Ages. For the named locations, Bartholomew described the inhabitants, with information about cities, the state of the soils, woods, rivers and lakes. The thoroughness of the material in the gazetteer reflects the practical needs of the friars to move through the material world.

On the Properties of Things devotes considerable attention to animals and other creatures, but it does so with an allegorical approach. An allegory is a concrete or material form that discloses an abstract or spiritual meaning. Medieval Christians were very interested in animals and other aspects of creation because they understood them to convey religious lessons. Bartholomew's treatment of bees illustrates his interest in nature's creatures, but also the profound differences between his allegorical approach and modern science. In book 12, on flying creatures, bees are presented as performing specific tasks in service to their king, modeling obedience for human beings. In book 17, bees are presented as industrious, working hard to create honey from flowers. Book 18 presents bees as part of the larger grouping of crawling creatures based on their property of using their legs as well as their wings. Book 19 described the products of bees that are useful to human beings: honey, honeyed wine, medicated honey, and beeswax for candles. These properties of bees all reinforce Bartholomew's fundamental instructional theme: be obedient to one's religious superior within a community; work hard; God's Word is sweet and fruitful; and allow one's sensory experience of nature to draw one into intimacy with God.[46] Bartholomew devoted a considerable effort to explaining nature and its creatures, and the religious lessons they

---

[46] Keen, *The Journey of a Book: Bartholomew the Englishman and the Properties of Things*, 32-34.

bear to human beings, especially to those aspiring to become preachers. Thus, nature and knowledge of nature was very important for Bartholomew and his friar students, but this allegorical presentation is quite different from the scientific methods we use today.

On the Properties of Things has been described as a medieval encyclopedia, because it presented foundational knowledge in a systematic way.[47] However, the best term to describe it is as a worldbook, for it conveyed in a relatively complete way critical knowledge one needed to live in the world, and the divinely inspired religious logic underneath its apparent chaos.[48] *On the Properties of Things* was among the most popular medieval worldbooks.[49] Late medieval editions in local languages were prized possessions of nobility. One scholar has suggested that the late medieval English translation of the book influenced Shakespeare, but this is speculative.[50] Thus, Bartholomew's book undertook its own journey, from the original hands of Franciscan students in Germany, to preachers seeking insight for opening up the Scriptures, to wealthy individuals seeking social status.

---

[47] The ancient scholars Pliny, Seneca and Isidore of Seville pioneered and developed the concept of the encyclopedia. See Michael W. Twomey, "Appendix: Medieval Encyclopedias," in *Medieval Christian Imagery: A Guide to Interpretation*, ed. R. E. Kaske, Arthur Groos, and Michael W. Twomey (Toronto: University of Toronto Press, 1988).

[48] The purpose of the worldbook was similar to that of medieval maps (mappamundi) and bestiaries (books describing animals). Christel Meier, "Organisation of Knowledge and Encyclopaedic Ordo: Functions and Purposes of a Universal Literary Genre," in *Pre-Modern Encyclopaedic Texts. Proceedings of the Second Comers Congress, Groningen, 1-4 July 1996*, ed. Peter Binkley (Leiden: Brill, 1997).

[49] It was the most cited source for sermon aids during the late Middle Ages. It was almost a library in itself, which made it useful for preachers, and filled a gap between other sources of knowledge. Lidaka, "Bartholomaeus Anglicus in the Thirteenth Century."

[50] Se Boyar, "Bartolomeus and His Encyclopedia," 168-69.

THE CONTEMPORARY FRANCISCAN SIGNIFICANCE OF BARTHOLOMEW

Friar Bartholomew taught his fellow Franciscans with the best available scientific knowledge to prepare them for preaching. He presented medieval science systematically to explain the natural world and its religious and moral purpose.[51] To our modern eyes, *On the Property of Things* might appear to be simplistic, or fantastical and speculative, and distorted by religious moralizing. To read it in its own context, however, means to understand Bartholomew's vocation as a medieval Franciscan scholar. His work was as useful in its time as Wikipedia or Google is for us today.

Bartholomew understood the natural world to be morally and religiously significant, and he taught his friar-students to understand that. Bartholomew engaged the Aristotelian paradigm and presented this to his students. His book introduced thousands of Franciscan students to a systematic understanding of the natural world as God's creation.

Bartholomew taught medieval science to Franciscans. To understand his vocation as a Franciscan, one must appreciate the transformation of the Franciscan movement from the primitive fraternity of brothers who knew Francis personally to an institution dedicated to sharing his vision of Gospel life with the entire Church. The universal mission of the Franciscans required knowledge of the world: its composition, its forms, its inhabitants, its dynamism, and its religious and moral purposes. Franciscans would have to know the properties of the things in the world in order to understand God's activity in the world, in the Bible, particularly for the purposes of prayer and preaching.

Bartholomew's book reveals how a Franciscan scholar conveyed the importance of learning about nature. It provided knowledge of the natural world, and wove it into a worldview that assumed that material reality has religious and moral significance. In *The Soul's Journey into God*, Bonaventure described how the invisible things of God can be grasped

---

[51] Greetham, "The Concept of Nature in Bartolomaeus Anglicus," 665.

intellectually through our senses. Bartholomew wrote "that earthly things can lead us to an understanding of heavenly things and to reconciliation with God." For Francis, Bonaventure and Bartholomew, knowledge of creation leads us to love of God.

CHAPTER THREE

ROGER BACON
AND THE OXFORD FRANCISCAN SCHOOL

But the whole aim of philosophy is that the Creator
may be known through the knowledge of the creature,
to whom service may be rendered in a worship that
gives him honor, in the beauty of morals, and in the
integrity of useful laws, because of the reverence due
his majesty and the benefits of creation and preserva-
tion and of future happiness, so that men may live in
peace and justice in this life.

Roger Bacon, *Opus Majus*[52]

Friar Roger Bacon was the Franciscan who made the
greatest contribution to the development of modern science.
He made substantial contributions to the way medieval Europe thought about light and the earth, and how to justify
knowledge.[53] He articulated the conceptual foundation for
modern experimental science using the intellectual tools of
his day. He has been called the first scientist, but Aristotle
is more deserving of this term.[54] Rather, Roger Bacon was

---

[52] Roger Bacon, *Opus Majus*, trans. Robert Belle Burke (New York:
Russell & Russell, 1267/1962), Part 2, chapter 7, 49.

[53] Jeremiah Hackett, "Roger Bacon and the Sciences: Introduction,"
in *Roger Bacon and the Sciences: Commemorative Essays*, ed. Jeremiah
Hackett (Chicago: University of Chicago Press, 1997).

[54] Brian Clegg, *The First Scientist: A Life of Roger Bacon* (New
York: Carroll & Graff Publishers, 2003). The claim of "first scientist" is
problematic for many reasons, including the tendency toward hagiographic
accounts of early scientists.

the medieval scientist who developed methods of justifying knowledge that led to the scientific revolution.[55] At first glance, Roger's scientific research might seem a mismatch with Franciscan religious life, yet from another perspective, Roger's investigations into the natural world were fully consistent with Francis's belief in the goodness of creation. For Roger, like Bartholomew and Bonaventure, understanding nature is inherently good because through it, we can come to greater knowledge and love of God. Roger is the best-known member of the Oxford Franciscan School, a community of friar-scholars whose investigation of nature was integral to their Franciscan vocation.[56]

Franciscan friars arrived in England in 1224, without any material resources, and shortly afterward, some of them moved to Oxford. As young men began to join the fraternity, the friars attached themselves to the growing University of Oxford, where they encountered a leading figure in efforts to use the Aristotelian paradigm to advance medieval science: Robert Grosseteste. Here the original goal of providing Franciscan education took root within a medieval university that was famous for its commitment to investigating the natural world. For Roger, investigating light, the Earth, and mathematics was a religious activity. While Francis expressed his love for creation and its elements through song, the Oxford Franciscans expressed this through their scientific investigations.

Roger Bacon advanced medieval science in three fundamental areas. First, he made important contributions to the scientific study of light, vision, energy, and the physical pro-

---

[55] Many details of his life have been clouded by subsequent polemical debates unrelated to him as a historical person. See Amanda Power, "A Mirror for Every Age: The Reputation of Roger Bacon," *English Historical Review* 121, 492 (2006): 657-92.

[56] With the exception of Andrew G. Little's scholarship, few studies have considered how Roger's Franciscan identity might have influenced his work. See Andrew G. Little, *The Grey Friars in Oxford* (Oxford: Clarendon Press, 1891); Andrew G. Little, *Studies in English Franciscan History* (London: Longmans, Green & Co., 1916); A.G. Little, "The Franciscan School at Oxford in the 13th Century," *Archivum Franciscanum Historicum* 19 (1926): 803-74.

cesses of change in nature.[57] Second, he described the Earth and the heavens using mathematics and maps, and has been called the Father of Modern Geography.[58] However, Roger Bacon is best known for his insistence on testing the claims of others with evidence. He did not propose the scientific method, but he did lead medieval science closer to modern science than any other natural philosopher.[59] This chapter presents his Franciscan vocation in the context of the Oxford Franciscan School, followed by some examples of Roger's medieval science, and a discussion of his significance today.

ROGER BACON'S FRANCISCAN VOCATION

Roger Bacon's religious life and work was touched by major currents in the religious, intellectual, and scientific developments of thirteenth-century Europe. Key elements in his biography are still in dispute, although his writings are not.[60] He appears to have been born in 1220, but he may have been born as early as 1214.[61] He appears to have entered the University of Oxford about 1228, receiving his M.A. about 1236. It was here that Roger met Robert Grosseteste, who would have a profound influence on him and the trajectory of the Franciscan intellectual tradition.

---

[57] Jeremiah Hackett, "Roger Bacon: His Life, Career and Works," in *Roger Bacon and the Sciences: Commemorative Essays*, ed. Jeremiah Hackett (Leiden: Brill, 1997), 12.

[58] This honorific title, from E.G.R. Taylor, "Compendium Cosmographiae: A Text-Book of Columbus," *Scottish Geographical Magazine* 47 (1931), is exaggerated, but has an element of truth, according to David Woodward and Herbert M. Howe, "Roger Bacon on Geography and Cartography," in *Roger Bacon and the Sciences*, ed. Jeremiah Hackettt (Leiden: Brill, 1997).

[59] Clegg, *The First Scientist: A Life of Roger Bacon.*

[60] For an overview of his writings, see Hackett, "Roger Bacon: His Life, Career and Works," 20-23. Clegg, *The First Scientist: A Life of Roger Bacon* lists 22 works by or attributed to Roger. See 221-24.

[61] Hackett, "Roger Bacon: His Life, Career and Works." Clegg, *The First Scientist: A Life of Roger Bacon.*

Robert Grosseteste (1168?-1253) was arguably the most influential English scholar of the thirteenth century.[62] He was a leader of the University of Oxford, serving as its chancellor on behalf of the Bishop of Lincoln. Robert led Oxford's intellectual life for two decades, until his election as Bishop of Lincoln in 1235. His approach dominated Oxford medieval science for the next two centuries.[63] Robert had a broad scope of interest: Biblical scholarship, natural philosophy, sermons, and preaching.[64] He translated and interpreted the newly rediscovered works of Aristotle; articulated a more sophisticated description of the physics of light; drew from mathematics to describe the behavior of light in optical lenses and rainbows, and nature more generally; and studied Greek and Hebrew so as to read the Bible and philosophy in their original languages.[65]

The friars were fortunate to recruit Robert Grosseteste as their teacher in 1229, and together they founded what would become the Oxford Franciscan School. Robert was attracted to the Gospel life of the Franciscans, and they invited him to be their chief teacher.[66] Robert introduced to the English Province of Franciscans a systematic approach to scholarship, including Aristotelian natural philosophy and practical investigations of nature, as a religious ideal.[67] He believed that learning should serve the Church and the evangelization of society. Roger Bacon described Robert Grosseteste as the most influential figure in his life,[68] and Robert may have encouraged Roger to join the Franciscans. Some evidence

---

[62] J. A. Weisheipl, "Science in the Thirteenth Century," in *The History of the University of Oxford*, ed. James I. Cato (Oxford: The Clarendon Press, 1984), 435-71.

[63] Weisheipl, "Science in the Thirteenth Century," 440.

[64] James McEvoy, *Robert Grosseteste* (New York: Oxford University Press, 2000), 9.

[65] Weisheipl, "Science in the Thirteenth Century," 442-43. Robert wrote extensively on these subjects: "On Light," "On Color," "On the Rainbow," and "On the Heat of the Sun." See French and Cunningham, *Before Science: The Invention of the Friars' Natural Philosophy*.

[66] McEvoy, *Robert Grosseteste*, 55.

[67] Weisheipl, "Science in the Thirteenth Century."

[68] Hackett, "Roger Bacon: His Life, Career and Works." Whether Roger Bacon was actually a student in Robert's classes is debatable.

suggests Robert considered joining the Franciscans prior to his appointment as Bishop of Lincoln.[69] Roger's intellectual development reflected Robert Grosseteste's vision ofscholarship in service of the Gospel. Robert's final gesture was to bequeath his library to the Franciscan friars.[70]

Roger went to the University of Paris about 1245, and taught there for roughly a decade. He became a Franciscan friar there in 1256, although he did not provide an explanation for his decision. He participated in the scholarly debates coursing through the University of Paris during subsequent decades. While there, he met Cardinal Guy Le Gros de Foulques. They spoke about Roger's vision of science and education, and their role in the reform of Church and society. Cardinal Guy was elected Pope Clement VI in 1265, and asked Roger to write his vision down in a book and send it to him.[71] This became known as the *Opus Majus* (in English, "Major Work"), and it captures Roger's vision of scientific research and teaching in service of Church and society. No biographical information exists for the last fifteen years of Roger's life, although he is believed to have returned to Oxford about 1278.[72] He continued to write, especially about the reform of education for the sake of Christianity and society, inspired until the end by Robert Grosseteste. He died in 1292.

The Oxford Franciscan School was one branch within the broader Franciscan intellectual tradition, and Robert Grosseteste and Roger Bacon are its premier examples.[73] The Ox-

---

[69] McEvoy, *Robert Grosseteste*, 55. Robert also had close relations with the Dominican friars.

[70] McEvoy, *Robert Grosseteste*, 55.

[71] David C. Lindberg, "Introduction," in *Roger Bacon's Philosophy of Nature: A Critical Edition of De Multiplicatione Specierum and De Speculis Comburentibus*, ed. David C. Lindberg (South Bend: St. Augustines Press, 1998).

[72] Jeremiah Hackett, "Roger Bacon on the Classification of the Sciences," in *Roger Bacon and the Sciences*, ed. Jeremiah Hackett (Leiden: Brill, 1997), 20.

[73] Some other examples are Adam Marsh and William of Ockham, but there were others as well. See Little (1916), 193 ff. John Duns Scotus may be considered influenced by the Oxford School, but he did not share the same degree of interest in natural philosophy or empirical studies as did Roger.

ford Franciscan School shared with friars at the University of Paris a commitment to Franciscan philosophy and theology, but the Oxford friars pursued this through the study of light, nature, and mathematical measurement.[74] Friar-scholars at both universities further developed Franciscan thought about nature, and these two schools indicate some of the diversity within the Franciscan intellectual tradition. Bonaventure, as an example of the friars at Paris, emphasized philosophy, theology and mysticism, while Roger, as an example of the Franciscans at Oxford, emphasized natural philosophy, direct observation of nature, and theology. Both approaches are valid, and both are needed to represent the breadth of the Franciscan intellectual tradition.

LIGHT, EARTH AND METHOD

Roger wrote the *Opus Majus* for Pope Clement VI as an appeal to fund his program in natural philosophy and science. Roger was convinced these were essential to reform and defend Christianity. An enormous handwritten document of some half a million words, the *Opus Majus* captures the breadth of subjects that Roger thought essential. It provided an impressive synthesis of existing knowledge in philosophy, languages, mathematics, theology, ethics, the science of light, geography, and methods for investigating natural phenomena.

Roger contributed three key ideas to medieval science which would become essential features in modern science. First, he insisted on the importance of direct observation and argument from evidence. He did this in an era when most natural philosophers restated the opinions from ancient and recent scholars, known as argument from authority. Second, he demonstrated the importance of quantitative reasoning, using applied mathematics and geometry. Roger had a very strong mathematical orientation, and the *Opus Majus*

---

[74] French and Cunningham, *Before Science: The Invention of the Friars' Natural Philosophy*, 230.

is filled with geometrical diagrams and arguments. Third, he argued the importance of testing the claims of others, at times using technological instruments, to justify knowledge. Roger used the Latin term *scientia experimentalis*, but as will be seen below, he did not mean a scientific experiment in the modern sense.

It was from Robert Grosseteste that Roger Bacon learned a love of light. For them, light meant more than it does for us. Light is how God created the world. Light is at the heart of creation itself. Light connected the human eye with the rest of creation. For them, light itself was a creative force, and by studying its behavior in the world, they could come to understand God and God's actions in a deeper way. Roger expressed his love of light thus:

> If the consideration just mentioned [mathematics] is noble and pleasing, the one in hand is far nobler and more pleasing, since we take especial delight in vision, and light and color have a special beauty beyond the other things that are brought to our senses, and not only does beauty shine forth but also [optics and light] bring benefits and answer to a great need. ... It is possible that some other science may be more useful, but no other science has so much sweetness and beauty of utility. Therefore, it is the flower of the whole philosophy and through it, and now without it, can the other sciences be known.[75]

Light was God in operation: the visible universe was light or the product of light; it was visible through the operation of light; it was intellectually graspable because the intellect too operated through light, and proper knowledge was illumination. Light was completely central to Roger's view of wisdom and how it is acquired.

Roger investigated light's reflection and refraction using geometric analysis and crude prisms, lenses, and mirrors. He used geometry to explain why straight sticks appeared

---

[75] *Opus majus*, part 5, distinction 1, chapter 1, transl. Clegg, 58-59.

to curve in water. His research into rainbows is the clearest example of what he meant by *scientia experimentalis*. He argued that claims by prior authorities should be tested with direct observation and measurement, which is what he did. He used prisms to generate small rainbows, and measured the behavior of light to explain their effects. He used geometry to accurately determine the maximum measured height of a natural rainbow in the sky at forty-two degrees, and was the first ever to do so. He described the workings of a telescope, and apparently had the materials to create a crude prototype, although there is no evidence that he actually did.[76]

Understanding the eye and its behavior was essential to understanding light. Roger used geometry to describe the anatomy of the human eye and the behavior of light within it. He described what we know as the retina, the cornea, and the optic nerves. He did not conduct dissection, but he applied his skills in geometry to existing knowledge of the eye.[77]

Roger's understanding of light and the eye is fundamentally different from ours today. He followed the ancient belief that light originates in the eye and radiates out to make perception possible, and then returns to be perceived by the eye.[78] For Roger, light was a unifying theory of matter: how it was created and how it changed through time, and how it linked human beings to the created world. Late medieval scientists, influenced by Roger's work, understood light to multiply as it moved through space. Four centuries later, Christiaan Huygens would develop the wave theory of light which supplanted Roger's ideas. In twenty-first century terms, Roger was pursuing the character of energy, or the dynamics of change within the physical universe, and was moved to do so by religious aspirations.

---

[76] David C. Lindberg, "Roger Bacon on Light, Vision, and the Universal Emanation of Force," in *Roger Bacon and the Sciences*, ed. Jeremiah Hackett (Leiden: Brill, 1997), 270; Clegg, *The First Scientist: A Life of Roger Bacon*, 44, 48, 199.

[77] Lindberg, "Roger Bacon on Light, Vision, and the Universal Emanation of Force," 256.

[78] Lindberg, "Roger Bacon on Light ...," 260 ff.

Roger applied mathematics and geometry to investigate the Earth and sky. Greek philosophers had understood the Earth as a sphere as far back as 500 BCE, but a few early Fathers of the Church, interpreting some Biblical passages literally, described the Earth as a flat disk. Most medieval natural philosophers understood the Earth as a sphere.[79] To justify this assertion, Roger wrote:

> We know by experience that he who is at the top of the mast can see the port more quickly than a man on the deck of the ship. Therefore it remains that something hinders the vision of the man on the deck of the ship. But there can be nothing but the swelling of the sphere of water.[80]

In a flat world, the man on the deck would see the port at the same time as the one at the top of the ship mast. The curvature of the Earth obscured his vision, but the man up the mast could see over this to land. Thus, the Earth must be a sphere.

Roger is considered the father of modern cartography because he applied mathematics to the creation of maps. He devised the most sophisticated approach to plotting location on them of the medieval era. Prior maps were artistic or allegorical representations of the Earth.[81] Roger called for a more systematic approach to mapping the world with contemporary technologies (astrolabe and compass) and geometry.[82] He devised a terrestrial coordinate system with latitude and longitude lines. His mathematical reasoning about the problems of representing a spherical Earth on flat paper laid the conceptual foundation for modern map projections.

---

[79] Clegg, *The First Scientist: A Life of Roger Bacon*, 155.

[80] Roger Bacon, *Opus Majus*, part 4, distinction 4, chapter 10. See discussion in Clegg, 156.

[81] Navigation charts were somewhat more sophisticated in that they relied upon the use of compass and referenced the stars; Roger contributed cosmography, or mapping of the stars, as well. Clegg, *The First Scientist: A Life of Roger Bacon*, 157.

[82] Woodward and Howe, "Roger Bacon on Geography and Cartography," 220.

Roger did not actually create a map projection, but his method of plotting points and locating them within a coordinate system was a remarkable innovation for his time in scientifically representing geographic space.

Relative to other medieval scholars interested in geography, Roger was more interested in the practical value of knowing the Earth. For example, he drew from the eyewitness accounts of Franciscan Friar William of Rubruck's travels to the Khan, the leader of the Tartars. William had travelled by land 1253-5 to a region near present day Mongolia as an ambassador for Louis IX, King of France.[83] William was one of several friars who undertook diplomatic missions during this period. Roger apparently met him in person, and they shared a Franciscan orientation toward mission, a curiosity about distant lands, and a commitment to understanding other peoples who were an armed threat to Christian Europe. He proposed that Asia could be reached by sailing west using his terrestrial coordinate system.[84]

He applied mathematics to calculating the position of the stars and the movement of comets. He proposed an explanation for why stars twinkle. He described climatic zones, and how they influenced the peoples who lived in them. He conceived several innovative technologies: a device for humans to explore the bottom of the sea, a flying machine, and a self-powered carriage for land travel. He did little more than identify these as ideas, and it would take more than six centuries before these technologies could be successfully engineered.[85]

Roger articulated three reasons to expand geographical knowledge. First, it leads to an understanding of the infinite heavens. To be interested in heaven requires one to understand the Earth and to map the universe, a field known as cosmography. Second, the Bible is full of geographical features; thus location, space, and geography are essential to understanding the Bible. His third reason distinguished

[83] Louis IX is the co-patron of the Secular Franciscan Order.
[84] Woodward and Howe, "Roger Bacon on Geography and Cartography," 202, and Clegg, *The First Scientist: A Life of Roger Bacon*, 158-60.
[85] Clegg, *The First Scientist: A Life of Roger Bacon*, 42 ff.

Roger from his contemporaries. He insisted upon a systematic, mathematical way of mapping the location of places for the practical needs of government, to understand history and to predict from whence the threats to Christianity were likely to come.[86] Roger appealed to Pope Clement IV to recognize and financially support more research into the systematic knowledge of the Earth, for the good of the Church.[87] The *Opus Majus* was a proposal for funding research to advance this scientific field, although there is no evidence that the Pope ever read it.

For all his work in light, vision, and geography, Roger Bacon is best known for laying the foundation for the modern scientific method. Other medieval scientists deployed observation and mathematics, but it is Roger who clearly articulated the importance of testing the factual claims of others using direct observation and measurement. Roger advocated *scientia experimentalis*, and demonstrated what he meant through his research into light. This term has been translated as "experimental science," but this is not accurate. Roger does not describe a modern understanding of a scientific experiment, with a hypothesis and conclusion. What Roger meant is probably best conveyed as "the experience of observation to test the claims of others." Roger made systematic observations of natural phenomena, which he described carefully in his writings. He critiqued the common medieval practice of mimicking what others had merely claimed to be true, which is exactly what Bartholomew the Englishman had done in *On the Properties of Things*. Roger Bacon advanced medieval science by articulating a more rigorous approach to the justification of knowledge, and thus laid the conceptual foundation for the modern scientific method.

The *Opus Majus* conveys Roger's epistemology, his understanding of how we are to create new knowledge, and why we should do this in particular ways.[88] Roger applied his philoso-

---

[86] Woodward and Howe, "Roger Bacon on Geography and Cartography," 204.

[87] David Woodward, "Roger Bacon's Terrestrial Coordinate System," *Annals of the Association of American Geographers* 80, no. 1 (1990): 117.

[88] Hackett, "Roger Bacon on the Classification of the Sciences," 59.

phy of knowledge to the improvement of teaching. He argued
that Aristotelian science should be used by theologians to create a more vital moral philosophy and theology. He believed
there were serious deficiencies in the educational system of
the time, and that this hindered the work of the Church.[89]
Roger was especially concerned with the reform of theological education for preachers, which he thought should include
science.[90] Roger Bacon believed that the study of geometry
and light was essential to the pursuit of wisdom. He believed
that deficient studies had led to deficient preaching, and to
the corruption of society. Thus, by reforming education, one
would reform Christianity.[91] Roger's vision of learning and
science reflects a certain Franciscan idealism. Even though
he did not use mystical or passionate language, Roger Bacon's life and work show how, in the Franciscan tradition,
knowledge is for love.

THE CONTEMPORARY FRANCISCAN SIGNIFICANCE OF ROGER BACON

Moving from Francis of Assisi to Roger Bacon shifts our
focus from poetic inspiration to scientific investigation. The
thrust of the Franciscan intellectual tradition emphasizes

---

[89] Roger was very critical of his contemporaries who did not see things
the same way. One late medieval source describes Roger Bacon as being
"condemned" between 1277 and 1279 by Jerome of Ascoli, the General
Minister of the Franciscan Friars, "on account of certain suspected
novelties." Some believe he was imprisoned by the friars. However, this has
been effectively disproved by recent scholarship. The source reporting his
condemnation is *The Chronicle of Twenty-four Generals*, written a century
after the events described. See David C. Lindberg, "Introduction," in *Roger
Bacon's Philosophy of Nature: A Critical Edition of De Multiplicatione
Specierum and De Speculis Comburentibus* (South Bend: St. Augustines
Press, 1998), especially discussion on pages xxv-xxvi, in which Lindberg
argues that Roger's imprisonment described in *The Chronicle of Twenty-
four Generals* is highly suspect.

[90] Timothy J. Johnson, "Preaching Precedes Theology: Roger Bacon on
the Failure of Mendicant Education," *Franciscan Studies* 68 (2010): 83-97.

[91] Lindberg, "Roger Bacon on Light, Vision, and the Universal
Emanation of Force."

continuity of the Franciscan spirit through entering the institutions of society, such as universities. Roger Bacon engaged and advanced the "new" medieval Aristotelian paradigm. He proposed new ways of investigating the natural world and of organizing education. Roger's creative and brilliant studies, representing the best of the Oxford Franciscan School, manifest a fascination with nature and its significance. Roger did not explicitly refer to Francis as an inspiration, yet his concern for nature can be seen in continuity with Francis. Roger pursued an intimacy with nature through his studies and investigations. He considered the study of nature a religious act. The contributions of Roger Bacon illustrate the role of science in the Franciscan intellectual tradition.

The Oxford Franciscan School engaged the knowledge systems of the thirteenth century, especially the sciences. The foundations for modern scientific method were laid by medieval natural philosophers, and the Oxford Franciscans participated in its development.[92] They pursued study of the natural world because in so doing they would learn about God, and in the process, they helped lay the conceptual foundation for experimental science. The Oxford Franciscan School advanced natural philosophy and helped make possible the conditions necessary for the scientific revolution. They were leading thinkers of their age who worked with the new scientific paradigm of Aristotelian thought about nature, and transformed it into the foundation of modern scientific method.

The scientific investigations of the Oxford Franciscan School demonstrate their response to the fundamental questions about knowledge raised by the medieval Aristotelian paradigm: could nature be known independently of God? In prior centuries, this type of question did not arise because people thought about nature primarily in allegorical terms. During this era, this approach became unsatisfactory.

"Can nature be known independently of God?" is a classic question that challenges us today to think about the relative

---

[92] Grant, *The Foundations of Modern Science in the Middle Ages: Their Religious, Institutional, and Intellectual Contexts.*

value of scientific understanding within the Catholic tradition. Science has dramatically expanded our understanding of life in our universe. Modern science has acted like a spotlight, illuminating areas of knowledge that previously had been shrouded in mystery. This has made some religious people uncomfortable, and in some cases, suspicious of science and scientists. This is most unfortunate; if one assumes that religion and science are incompatible, faith becomes compartmentalized, and disconnected from broader concerns within society. If faith is focused only on the miraculous, one turns away from the hopes and concerns of our brothers and sisters in the world. To split scientific and religious ways of viewing the world results in alienation and fragmentation, and undermines the potential to present God's love in a way that contemporary people can understand. The Oxford Franciscan School would find such an approach incomprehensible, and it is inconsistent with the Franciscan intellectual tradition.

What we would today recognize as science was built upon the philosophical and intellectual foundation laid down by theologian-natural philosophers such as Roger. Much of the history of science has been written in such a way that it erases the contribution of the religious scholars of the Middle Ages.[93] This academic work was sponsored by Church institutions, especially religious orders, as a religious activity. Historians of science have tended to disregard the contribution of church-affiliated people, because many of them assume that the Catholic Church played a corrupting or obstructing role in the development of modern science, or that it promotes superstition.[94] Some of the more recent and balanced historical accounts have reevaluated the scientific revolution in light of this contribution of medieval theologian-natural philosophers.[95] Yet there is almost no scholarship that has examined the role that natural philosophy played in the development

---

[93] David C. Lindberg, "Medieval Science and Its Religious Context," *Osiris* 10 (1995), 60-79.

[94] Lindberg, "Medieval Science ...," 60-79.

[95] Grant, *The Foundations of Modern Science in the Middle Ages: Their Religious, Institutional, and Intellectual Contexts.*

of religious orders, including the Franciscans.[96] Few Franciscans today realize the importance of the contribution of these early Franciscan scholars, and as a result, few Franciscans today realize the breadth of impact on Church and society that this religious movement had.

Roger Bacon and the Oxford Franciscan School were at the forefront of medieval science. Roger's natural philosophy and investigations should be understood as a part of his (Franciscan) religious project, his faith. Can we today recognize Roger Bacon as genuinely "Franciscan"? In other words, can we perceive Roger as faithful to Francis's vision? The scientific inquiry of the Oxford Franciscan School invites us today to ask ourselves: what is the role of studying nature for us today? Can we recognize the study of science and nature as a religious activity?

---

[96] One exception is French and Cunningham, *Before Science: The Invention of the Friars' Natural Philosophy*.

Chapter Four

Bernardino de Sahagún:
Missionary-Anthropologist in New Spain

In order to give examples and make comparisons, in
the preaching of the Gospel, knowledge of the things
of nature is certainly not the least noble jewel in the
treasury. We see the Redeemer as having used it. ...
To this end, with much labor and work, this volume,
a compendium, was made. In it, recorded in the Mexican language, are the better known and most utilized
animals, birds, fish, trees, herbs, flowers, and fruits
which exist in all this land – their characteristic properties and traits, exterior and interior. In it there is a
great abundance of words and many current expressions, very correct and very common, very pleasing
material.

Bernardino de Sahagún,
La Historia General de las Cosas de Nueva España[97]

Bernardino was a Franciscan friar, missionary priest and
pioneering anthropologist participating in the Catholic evangelization of colonial New Spain (now Mexico). He was born
in what is now Spain in 1499, travelled to New Spain in 1529,
and spent more than fifty years interviewing Aztecs and

---

[97] Bernardino de Sahagún, *Florentine Codex: General History of the
Things of New Spain (Translation of and Introduction to Historia General
De Las Cosas De La Nueva España; 12 Volumes in 13 Books)*, trans. Charles
E. Dibble and Arthur J. O Anderson (Salt Lake City: University of Utah
Press, 1950-1982), Prologue to Book XI, in the Introductory Volume, 87.

documenting their religious beliefs, culture and knowledge of nature. His primary motivation was to evangelize indigenous Mesoamerican peoples, and most of his writings were devoted to this end. However, his extraordinary research documenting the Aztec indigenous worldview and culture has earned him the title "the first anthropologist."[98]

Bernardino is best known as the author of *La Historia General de las Cosas de Nueva Espana* (in English: the *General History of the Things of New Spain*), hereafter *Historia General*. It consists of twelve "books" of 2,400 pages, with 2,000 vivid illustrations painted by native artists, many in color.[99] The *Historia General* reported his anthropological research, conducted with his former students, to interpret for European Christians: Aztec gods, religious worldview, ritual practices, culture, and economy, plus the animals, plants and environment of Mesoamerica.[100] Copies were carried to the royal court of Spain and to the Vatican. He was first and foremost a missionary who sought to evangelize the Aztecs, but he used his intellectual and scientific gifts to improve mutual understanding across cultural differences. Bernardino wrote and revised several editions of the *Historia General* until his death in 1590.

The *Historia General* was "lost" for several centuries until it was rediscovered in a library in Florence, Italy, and is now commonly referred to as *The Florentine Codex*. One scholar described the *Historia General* as "one of the most remarkable accounts of a non-Western culture ever composed."[101] Bernardino's most impressive contribution was his pioneering methodology, for he created new forms of gathering

---

[98] Miguel León-Portilla, *Bernardino De Sahagún: The First Anthropologist* (Norman: University of Oklahoma Press, 2002).

[99] To see examples of these color pictures, consult the Wikipedia entry on The Florentine Codex.

[100] Bernardino described the *Historia General* as an explanation of the "divine, or rather idolatrous, human, and natural things of New Spain." Prologue to Book XI, Introductory Volume, 46.

[101] H. B. Nicholson, "Fray Bernardino De Sahagún: A Spanish Missionary in New Spain, 1529-1590," in *Representing Aztec Ritual: Performance, Text, and Image in the Work of Sahagún*, ed. Eloise Quiñones Keber (Boulder: University of Colorado Press, 2002).

knowledge and justifying it. This chapter begins with an overview of Bernardino's Franciscan vocation as academic and missionary. This is followed by a description of his research project and methodology. The contemporary implications of his scientific work conclude the chapter.

Bernardino's Vocation as a Franciscan Missionary

Bernardino attended the University of Salamanca, in Spain, which exposed him to the currents of Renaissance humanism, a philosophy of education that sought to create well-rounded and virtuous citizens. This era at Salamanca was strongly influenced by the thought of Erasmus, and was a center for Spanish Franciscan intellectual life. He joined the Franciscan friars there.[102] His academic and religious reputation was strong, and thus he was recruited to travel to New Spain as a missionary.[103] He would spend the rest of his sixty-one years there.

The discovery of the "New World" prompted a surge of interest in missionary evangelization among Catholics. This work was often sponsored by royalty, especially the kings and queens of Catholic Spain and Portugal. Missionary efforts were woven together with European conquest and colonization projects. The conquistador Hernán Cortez conquered Tenochtitlan (on the site of present day Mexico City) in 1521, resulting in violence, social chaos, and lots of bloody fighting over plunder among the conquistadores. The first Franciscan friars arrived shortly afterward. The contradictions between conquering people of other cultures and preaching the Good News to them were generally ignored by Europeans during this era.

The evangelization of New Spain was led by Franciscan, Dominican and Augustinian friars.[104] These religious orders

---

[102] León-Portilla, *Bernardino De Sahagún: The First Anthropologist*.

[103] León-Portilla, *Bernardino De Sahagún: The First Anthropologist*.

[104] Jaime Lara, *City, Temple, Stage: Eschatological Architecture and Liturgical Theatrics in New Spain* (South Bend: University of Notre Dame, 2005).

established the Catholic Church in colonial New Spain, and directed it for most of the sixteenth century. The Franciscans in particular were enthralled with this new land and its people. The decades after the Spanish conquest witnessed a dramatic transformation of indigenous culture, with many experiences of violence, subjugation and oppression. At the same time, there was a religious dimension of this transformation, which contributed to the creation of a new cultural reality in what is now Mexico.[105] People from both the Spanish and Indigenous cultures held a wide range of opinions and views about what was happening during this transformation. Some Spanish conquistadores were quite brutal toward the Indigenous people, others somewhat humane.

The Franciscan friars who came to the "New World" were motivated by a desire to preach the Gospel to new peoples.[106] They were convinced that there was great religious meaning in the encounter with these new peoples.[107] Many friars were discontented with the corruption of European society, including some leaders of the Church, and saw New Spain as an opportunity to revive the pure spirit of primitive Christianity. During the first decades of the Spanish conquest of Mesoamerica, enormous numbers of indigenous peoples converted to Catholicism, or at least were baptized by the friars. The initial stages of the colonial evangelization project appeared quite successful, despite outbreaks of violence and the extraordinary greed of the conquistadores.

The indigenous people did not follow through in practicing their new Christian faith as the missionary friars expected of them. Many of them continued their ancestral Aztec religious rituals even as they participated in Catholic wor-

[105] Robert Ricard, *The Spiritual Conquest of Mexico* (Berkeley: University of California Press, 1966).

[106] Edwin Edward Sylvest, *Motifs of Franciscan Mission Theory in Sixteenth Century New Spain Province of the Holy Gospel* (Washington DC: Academy of American Franciscan History, 1975).

[107] They thought that preaching to them would bring about the return of Christ and the end of time, which was a form of millenarianism. See John Leddy Phelan, *The Millennial Kingdom of the Franciscans in the New World* (Berkeley: University of California Press, 1970). Also, Lara, *City, Temple, Stage*.

ship. The Spanish friars had disagreements over how best to approach this problem. Franciscans typically hold a diversity of views, but in this case, the stakes were quite high and the social context volatile, at times violent. The friars were very far away from the Spanish royal courts and European religious authorities, and there was very little understanding in Europe of what life was like in the colonies. To a modern person, the persistence of centuries-old religious practices among new Christians seems unsurprising. But the Indigenous people of the New World were of a culture completely incomprehensible to Europeans. The lack of understanding of Aztec culture on the part of Spanish conquistadores and friars led to violent conflicts and injustices in New Spain.

Bernardino helped found the first European school of higher education in the Americas, which would serve as a base for his research activities.[108] The Spanish authorities funded and he cofounded the Colegio Imperial de Santa Cruz de Tlatelolco (the Imperial College of the Holy Cross at Tlatelolco) in 1536, in what is now Mexico City.[109] The school had two purposes: the Franciscans would train the sons of Aztec nobility for the priesthood, and the friars would study native languages in preparation for evangelization. The school at Tlatelolco was important for the establishment of Catholic christianity in New Spain, but it also became an important institution for cultural exchange.

Bernardino taught Latin and other subjects.[110] Other friars taught grammar, history, religion, scripture, and philosophy. In addition, native leaders were recruited to teach native history and traditions, which would later stir controversy among conquistadores and colonial officials concerned with controlling indigenous peoples.[111] Bernardino was just one of

---

[108] Francisco Borgia Steck, OFM, *El Primer Colegio De America: Santa Cruz De Tlatelolco* (Mexico: Centro de Estudios Franciscanos, 1944).

[109] León-Portilla, *Bernardino De Sahagún: The First Anthropologist*; Michael Mathes, *The Americas' First Academic Library: Santa Cruz De Tlatelolco* (Sacramento: California State Library, 1985); and Borgia Steck, *El Primer Colegio De America: Santa Cruz De Tlatelolco*.

[110] Nicholson, "Fray Bernardino De Sahagún: A Spanish Missionary in New Spain, 1529-1590."

[111] León-Portilla, *Bernardino De Sahagún: The First Anthropologist*.

several friars at the school who would go on to write impressive accounts of indigenous life and culture.[112] Franciscans in New Spain who affirmed the full humanity of indigenous people were perceived as suspicious by colonial officials, and some hinted that they endorsed idolatry. Pro-indigenous friars had to be very careful as to how they described their interactions with the Aztecs. Of course, since these friars were the most proficient in Aztec language, they had a much greater grasp of the indigenous culture – and the activities of the native peoples – than did the colonial officials.

The school functioned as a meeting place between Spanish and indigenous cultures. Two notable "products" of the school were the first New World herbal, and the first colonial map of what is now the Mexico City region. An herbal is a catalogue of plants and their uses, including descriptions and their medicinal applications. The plants were drawn, named and presented according to the Aztec system of organization, but in Latin. It described where the plants grow and how they can be prepared for use as herbal medicines. It may have been used to teach indigenous medicine at the school.[113] The map shows the urban areas, networks of roads and canals, pictures of activities such as fishing and farming, and the broader landscape context. The herbal and the map display clear influence of Spanish and Aztec cultures; they convey by their structure and style the blending of these cultures.[114]

In addition to teaching, Bernardino spent several extended periods during the 1540s outside of the colonial capital

---

[112] Munro S. Edmonson, ed., *Sixteenth-Century Mexico: The Work of Sahagún* (Albuquerque, New Mexico: University of New Mexico Press, 1974).

[113] Juan Badianus de la Cruz was an Aztec teacher at the college, and presumed to be the chief author, but likely had help from students or other teachers. The Badianus de la Cruz Herbal was written in Latin. William Gates, *An Aztec Herbal: The Classic Codex of 1552* (Mineola, New York: Dover Publications, 1939/2000). Donald Robertson, *Mexican Manuscript Painting of the Early Colonial Period* (New Haven: Yale University Press, 1959), 155-63.

[114] It is known as the Mapa de Santa Cruz. See Robertson, *Mexican Manuscript Painting of the Early Colonial Period*, 155-63.

to evangelize, lead religious services, and provide religious instruction. Bernardino was first and foremost a missionary, motivated to bring the peoples of the New World to the Catholic faith. Bernardino was an exceptional linguist. He had begun his study of Nahuatl, the Aztec language, with indigenous nobility sailing back from Spain across the Atlantic. Bernardino became among the most proficient Europeans in this language.[115] His earliest writings were translations of the Psalms, Gospels and a basic religious education manual into Nahuatl.[116]

His intellectual curiosity drew him, and his linguistic gifts allowed him to learn more about the worldview of the Aztecs. In 1547, he collected formal speeches given by Aztec elders to young people for moral instruction.[117] Between 1553 and 1555 he interviewed indigenous leaders about the conquest of Mexico from their perspective.[118] He conducted this and all his research in the native language. Perhaps as a result of these initial investigations, he grew skeptical of the authenticity of the mass conversions of Aztecs. He thought many if not most of them were superficial. Perhaps more importantly, he became concerned about the tendency of his fellow Franciscan missionaries to misunderstand basic elements of traditional Aztec religious beliefs, worldview and culture. Bernardino became convinced that only by mastering native languages and worldviews could missionaries be effective.[119] He began to formalize new ways of conducting research into Aztec beliefs, religious practices, and worldview.

As the initial Franciscan optimism about mass conversions of Aztecs began to fade, other friars in New Spain realized that they needed to better understand the indigenous peoples. Bernardino's life changed dramatically in 1558 when the Franciscan Provincial Minister (leader) of New

---

[115] León-Portilla, *Bernardino De Sahagún: The First Anthropologist.*

[116] Nicholson, "Fray Bernardino De Sahagún: A Spanish Missionary in New Spain, 1529-1590."

[117] León-Portilla, *Bernardino De Sahagún: The First Anthropologist.*

[118] Nicholson, "Fray Bernardino De Sahagún: A Spanish Missionary in New Spain, 1529-1590."

[119] Nicholson, "Fray Bernardino De Sahagún: A Spanish Missionary in New Spain, 1529-1590."

Spain commissioned him to write in Nahuatl what he considered useful for the missionary project. He gave Bernardino broad latitude in his study of native language and culture, so that he could explain his findings to other friars.[120] This opened up the way to a more systematic and rigorous approach to gathering, analyzing, and justifying his knowledge of Aztec culture. He actively gathered data for about twenty-five years, and spent the last fifteen years of his life revising the *Historia General*. He died at the advanced age of 90.

BERNADINO'S ANTHROPOLOGICAL RESEARCH

Bernardino's work can be understood as a multi-decade research project investigating a cluster of themes, expressed in several different forms, with religious, cultural and nature themes.[121] Bernardino's scientific work had three primary goals:

1. To describe and explain ancient indigenous religion, beliefs, practices, and deities. This was to help friars and others understand this "idolatrous" religion and to evangelize the Aztecs.
2. To create a vocabulary of the Aztec language, Nahuatl. This provided more than definitions from a dictionary; rather it included an explanation of their cultural origins, with pictures. This was to help friars and others learn Nahuatl and to understand the cultural context of the language.
3. To record and document the great cultural inheritance of the indigenous peoples of New Spain.[122]

---

[120] Nicholson, "Fray Bernardino De Sahagún: A Spanish Missionary in New Spain, 1529-1590."

[121] Edmonson, ed., *Sixteenth-Century Mexico: The Work of Sahagún*.

[122] From Alfredo López Austin, "The Research Method of Fray Bernardino De Sahagún: The Questionnaires," in *Sixteenth-Century Mexico: The Work of Sahagún*, ed. Munro S. Edmonson (Albuquerque: University of New Mexico Press, 1974), 121.

His field research activities can be grouped into an earlier period (1558-1561) and a later period (1561-1575).[123] His early work has been named *Primeros Memoriales* ("first memories").[124] This served as a pilot study prior to and became a template for the more ambitious *Historia General.*

Once he was commissioned in 1558 to write up his investigations, Bernardino moved back to Tepepolco, approximately fifty miles northeast of Mexico City, near present day Hidalgo, to get further away from the influence of other Spaniards. Bernardino spent two years interviewing elders of this village. He questioned them regarding their religious beliefs, rituals and calendar; family, economic and political behavior; and the plants, animals and environment. He interviewed these elders independently of each other, as well as in groups, in order to evaluate the validity of the information shared with him. During this period he pioneered and tested his own research methodologies.[125]

Throughout his investigations, Bernardino collaborated fully with Aztec graduates of the Colegio Imperial de Santa Cruz de Tlatelolco. These research associates spoke three languages (Nahuatl, Latin and Spanish), and actively shaped the research project and its methodologies over these decades. They helped with translation and interpretation, and they perhaps painted pictures. Bernardino described the contributions of these indigenous collaborators, naming them and assigning them credit, which was quite unusual for the time.[126] Between 1561 and 1575, Bernardino interviewed

---

[123] Alfredo López Austin, "The Research Method of Fray Bernardino De Sahagún: The Questionnaires," 121.

[124] Thelma D. Sullivan, *Primeros Memoriales: Paleography of Nahuatl Text and English Translation*, ed. Arthur J.O. Anderson with H.B. Nicholson, Charles E. Dibble, Eloise Quiñones Keber, and Wayne Ruwet, vol. 200, Civilization of the American Indian (Norman: University of Oklahoma Press, 1997).

[125] López Austin, "The Research Method of Fray Bernardino De Sahagún: The Questionnaires."

[126] He accorded more credit to Indigenous collaborators than any other sixteenth century colonial researcher. Arthur J. O Anderson, "Sahagún: Career and Character," in *Florentine Codex: Introductions and Indices*, ed. Arthur J. O Anderson and Charles E. Dibble (Salt Lake City: University of Utah Press, 1982).

additional elders in other communities, and expanded the scope of his study, which became the longer *Historia General*, in twelve volumes.[127]

> The twelve books of *La historia general de las cosas de Nueva España*[128]
> The Gods
> The Ceremonies
> The Origin of the Gods
> The Soothsayers
> The Omens
> Rhetoric and Moral Philosophy
> The Sun, Moon and Stars, and the Binding of the Years
> Kings and Lords
> The Merchants
> The People
> Earthly Things
> The Conquest

The *Historia General* is a complex manuscript, and some passages are contradictory. It reflects the process of assembling it over a period of decades, and Bernardino's multiple reasons for creating it. It captured the diversity of people that he and his associates interviewed, and the diversity of their opinions. Bernardino's goals of orienting fellow missionaries to Aztec culture, providing a rich Nahuatl vocabulary, and recording the indigenous cultural heritage at times compete with each other.

The 2,400 manuscript pages are generally of two columns. The right column is in Nahuatl, which was written first, and a subsequent Spanish translation or summary

---

[127] Robertson has argued that Bartholomew's worldbook served as a conceptual model for *Historia General*, although any evidence is circumstantial. D. Robertson, "The Sixteenth Century Mexican Encyclopedia of Fray Bernardino De Sahagún," *Journal of World History* 4 (1966).

[128] Bernardino de Sahagún, *Florentine Codex: General History of the Things of New Spain (Translation of and Introduction to Historia General De Las Cosas De La Nueva España; 12 Volumes in 13 Books)*. The sentences following the title are original subtitles.

translation, in the left column. Most of *Historia General* is text, but its 2,000 pictures provide vivid images of sixteenth-century New Spain.[129] Some pictures directly support the text, while others are thematically related; some only have a decorative purpose. Some are in vivid color; others are black and white sketches. The illustrations do not bear titles, and the relationship of some to the adjoining text is not always clear. They can be considered a "third column" in the *Historia General*. Several different artists' hands have been identified. The drawings convey a blend of indigenous and European artistic elements and cultural influences.[130]

Bernardino used numerous metaphors to explain his motivations for creating the *Historia General*. The text opens by comparing his work to that of a doctor: "the physician cannot advisedly administer medicines to the patient without first knowing ... from which source the ailment derives."[131] His meaning here was metaphorical, yet the *Historia General* demonstrated his special interest in Aztec understandings of anatomy, disease, and medicines. He seemed to invest more effort, and greater care, in this subject relative to others.

He gathered knowledge through a systematic approach to interviews using consistent questionnaires on specific themes, based on aspects of anatomy, disease, and medicine that he thought important. In book 10 chapter 27, he listed more than 3,000 Nahuatl anatomical terms for the human body. For example, he listed 125 Nahuatl terms used to describe teeth: their different types (e.g., molar, canine, and front teeth), and their color, shape and function.

Chapter 28 of book 10, titled "On the Illnesses of Our Body and their Corresponding Medicines, on What Constitutes their Medicine," identifies fifty-six illnesses of the human body. Examples include cysts, broken bones, and tooth

---

[129] To see full color examples of this art, please refer to the Wikipedia entry on the Florentine Codex.

[130] For analysis of the pictures and the artists, see several contributions to John Frederick Schwaller, ed., *Sahagún at 500: Essays on the Quincentenary of the Birth of Fr. Bernardino De Sahagún* (Berkeley: Academy of American Franciscan History, 2003).

[131] Prologue to Book I, in the Introductory Volume, 45.

infections. The presentation includes brief accounts of one or more of the necessary medicines, generally derived from plants. These provide information on the specific parts of the plant to be used, and where to find it. The entries for six of these illnesses provide recipes for how to prepare and administer the remedy. For example, the paragraph titled "lip sores" describes the illness and plant-based remedy thus:

> When just the sun, or the wind, or the cold have affected one, bee honey or [agave] syrup are put on; or drops of liquid rubber are spread on. But for the ailment of sore lips which comes from within, which comes to the surface of the lips, which is called an infection, one is to apply or put on [powdered] *tlatluahcapatli* [root]. And one is to clean the teeth with this [*tlatluahcapatli* and] with salt, and go on drinking this medicine.[132]

Other diseases and remedies include: for an infected ear, apply drops of a certain plant sap mixed with chili peppers three times daily; for head scabies, trim off all hair, wash the scalp with urine, and apply powdered avocado seeds, followed later by pine sap; for a fracture, place the broken bones in a splint, apply a poultice of herbs, and bathe it with agave wine. Six illnesses are identified without a cure. Chapter 28 provides twenty-seven paintings of doctors and patients, including some with medical instruments used to administer remedies to illnesses of the eye and hemorrhoids, such as obsidian scalpels. At the end of this chapter, eight "Mexican physicians" or native healers are identified as having "examined" (and presumably corrected) the text. Bernardino named his sources, and respected their knowledge.

Chapter 7 of book 11, titled "On Medicinal Plants and Diverse Herbs," identifies and describes 142 herb plants that are medicinal, functional, and edible. The information is presented consistently as though it were answers to the following questions:

---

[132] Book X, paragraph 1, 146.

1. What kind of plant is it?
2. What does it look like?
3. What are its useful parts?
4. Against what illnesses are they useful?
5. How is the medicine prepared?
6. How is it administered?
7. Where is it found?[133]

The entry for the plant named *tzompoton* exemplifies this:

It is an herb which forms many branches; they are green. Its leaves are long, small and wide, straight. Its blossoms are white. When it has blossomed, its blossoms are like feathers. Right there they are borne away by the wind.... Its root is bitter. There is just one – small and cylindrical, forked. It is small, one finger thick. On the surface it is white; it is yellow below. It is pounded with a stone, boiled, well cooked. It is required by one who is about to die of diarrhea, who cannot stop it, who just vomits up food. He drinks it; thus [the diarrhea] is quickly stopped. Just a little is to be drunk. And if a little child [is sick], it is to drink one or two mouthfuls to stop it. It grows everywhere, in the mountains, in the forest.[134]

This book goes on to describe remedies based on applying stones, animal meat, ground insects, and sweat baths. This book has a great number of highly detailed pictures of plants, which are still useful today for ethnobotany, the field of anthropology that investigates how indigenous people use plants for food and medicine. Bernardino devoted a great deal of time and effort to gathering Aztec knowledge of

---

[133] Alfredo López Austin, "Sahagún's Work and the Medicine of the Ancient Nahuas: Possibilities for Study," in *Sixteenth-Century Mexico: The Work of Sahagún*, ed. Munro S. Edmonson (Albuquerque: University of New Mexico Press, 1974), 211.

[134] Book XI, paragraph 5, 184.

health, disease and remedy, and apparently thought it had practical value.

Bernardino's questions to the Aztecs are similar to those that all humans ask about these subjects. We today want to know about all the parts of our body, their names and functions. We want to know about the symptoms and causes of our illnesses. We want to know about available remedies. He described how to differentiate between a good and a bad "doctors," and he evidently relied upon the expertise of the good ones.

Yet many of the ideas about diseases and remedies used by Bernardino and his contacts would be considered superstitious today. Some of the illnesses described in the *Historia General* were understood to have been caused beings from the spirit world, or the failure to properly uphold certain Aztec rituals. For example, he described Aztec gods who, wanting specific women to serve as their escorts, brought a specific form of death. Bernardino reported Aztec offerings to appease gods, and the use of amulets for healing. Some of these are found in early drafts, and were considered too idolatrous, or perhaps pagan, and were edited out.[135]

Bernardino's document is remarkable not because he sometimes criticized the beliefs of others as idolatrous, but rather, for reporting so much information reflecting the Aztec worldview that most other Europeans would have dismissed out of hand, perhaps as witchcraft. The *Historia General*'s treatment of health and disease is all the more intriguing because Bernardino invested so much effort in this area. Did he himself ever take advantage of these remedies? Although we have not evidence that he did, the level of interest he demonstrated in this suggests that he might have considered doing so.

Bernardino was among the first to develop a diverse set of strategies for gathering and validating knowledge of indigenous New World cultures. In the context of significant uncertainty among Spaniards about Aztec culture, Bernardino

---

[135] López Austin, "Sahagún's Work and the Medicine of the Ancient Nahuas: Possibilities for Study," 206.

created new ways to gather, document, and justify the human knowledge of others. Thus, his work can be considered an early form of social science. Centuries later, the scientific discipline of anthropology would later formalize his methodology as ethnography (the scientific research strategy to document the beliefs, behavior, social roles and relationships, and worldview of another culture, but to explain these within the logic of that culture). Ethnographic tools can be used to investigate the knowledge systems of other social groups. Ethnography requires the practice of empathy with those very different from oneself, and the suspension of one's own cultural beliefs in order to understand and explain the worldview of those living in another culture. Even though Bernardino conducted his research prior to the modern scientific method, his research activities and his strategies for justifying knowledge shared by members of another culture demonstrate a substantial contribution to the thought of human society.

Bernardino systematically gathered knowledge from a range of diverse indigenous people who were recognized as having expert knowledge of Aztec culture. His methods for justifying knowledge demonstrate the following general principles.[136]

1. Use the native language (in this case, Nahuatl).
2. Dialogue with the cultural authorities who are publicly recognized as most knowledgeable (in this case, the elders).
3. The researcher should adapt him or herself to the ways in which the other culture records and transmits knowledge (in this case, oral commentaries and pictographs).
4. Use the expertise of others (in this case, graduates of his school).

---

[136] Adapted from Miguel León-Portilla, "Bernardino De Sahagún: Pioneer of Anthropology," in *Sahagún at 500: Essays on the Quincentenary of the Birth of Fr. Bernardino De Sahagún*, ed. John Frederick Schwaller (Berkeley: Academy of American Franciscan History, 2003).

5. Try to understand the totality or complete reality of the other culture on its own terms.

6. Use structured inquiry, such as a questionnaire, but be prepared to set it aside if valuable information is shared through other means.

7. Pay special attention to native languages and the diverse ways in which diverse meanings are transmitted through them.

8. Undertake a comparative evaluation of information from multiple sources in order to determine the degree of confidence with which one can hold that information.

These were Bernardino's strategies for investigating the Aztec knowledge system, and these methodological innovations substantiate the claim Bernardino was the first anthropologist.[137]

His last years were difficult; the idealism of the first Franciscans in New Spain was fading, the Spanish colonial project continued its brutality, and plagues took the lives of millions of Aztecs. Some of Bernardino's final writings disclose feelings of despair. The King of Spain replaced the religious orders with secular clergy, giving friars a much smaller role in the Catholic life of the colony. The Nahuatl Bible was banned, reflecting the broader retrenchment of Catholicism under the Council of Trent, and the pro-indigenous approach espoused by Bernardino and many of the Franciscans was largely discarded.

---

[137] Bernardino conducted his research in the context of a tumultuous period in which the conquering Spaniards were quite small in number relative to the Aztecs, and Colonial officials were quite concerned about the threat of an Indian uprising. Some perceived Bernardino's work to be dangerous, for his documentary project could afford legitimacy to native voices and perspectives. His work was originally conducted only in Nahuatl, and to fend off suspicion and criticism, he translated sections of it into Spanish. He was aware of the need to avoid running afoul of the inquisition, which was established in Mexico in 1570. Even though he had been commissioned by the leader of Franciscans in New Spain to do this work, ongoing tensions among his fellow Franciscans brought greater scrutiny and opposition within his own religious order. See León-Portilla, *Bernardino De Sahagún: The First Anthropologist*.

CONTEMPORARY FRANCISCAN SIGNIFICANCE OF BERNARDINO

Bernardino has been described as an ethnographer, linguist, folklorist, historian, and pro-indigenous, and he was all of these.[138] The *Historia General* was essentially lost for about two centuries, until a scholar "found" it in a library in Florence, Italy. A scholarly community of historians, anthropologists, art historians, and linguists has been actively investigating Bernardino's work, its subtleties and mysteries, for more than 200 years.[139] The *Historia General* is one of the most remarkable cultural research projects ever conducted.[140]

Other Spaniards documented life in the New World. Bernardino went beyond their work to develop novel methodologies to gather a wide range of cultural information and then weigh competing evidence, and thus to justify the validity of that knowledge. He considered the people important enough to spend decades researching them and their knowledge system in partnership with them. He cared enough to study the Aztec knowledge system on their own terms. He reported the worldview of people of Mesoamerica as they themselves understood it.

Scholars have proposed different explanations for his genius and creativity.[141] These dimensions of his identity are helpful for explaining his creativity and vision, but they do not fully explain his actions and innovations. An explanation may be found in his training as a Franciscan friar and

---

[138] Edmonson, ed., *Sixteenth-Century Mexico: The Work of Sahagún*.

[139] For a history of this scholarly work, see León-Portilla, *Bernardino De Sahagún: The First Anthropologist*.

[140] Nicholson, "Fray Bernardino De Sahagún: A Spanish Missionary in New Spain, 1529-1590," 27.

[141] Some have pointed to early Renaissance humanism he learned at the University of Salamanca. See León-Portilla, *Bernardino De Sahagún: The First Anthropologist*. Others have pointed to the Spanish missionary fervor for converting newly discovered peoples combined with the intellectual influence of the library at the *Colegio of Tlatelolco*. See Robertson, "The Sixteenth Century Mexican Encyclopedia of Fray Bernardino De Sahagún."

preacher, priest and teacher. Few studies reference the influence of his Franciscan vocation, and none investigate the
influence of Franciscan life on his work. His pro-indigenous
approach is certainly consistent with the spirit of compas-
sion embodied by St. Francis. The conquistadors viewed Aztecs as little more than animals, slaves, or at best, children.
Bernardino perceived them as human beings.

It is likely that Bernardino studied the works of John
Duns Scotus at the University of Salamanca before coming
to New Spain. The philosophy of Scotus reflects the intuitive
insights of St. Francis of Assisi and his devotion to the coming of Jesus Christ as a human being. Scotus developed these
intuitions into a formal philosophy of what it means to be a
human being, and how we are to live together in community.[142] In the context of great uncertainty and dramatic cultural change, a philosophical anthropology guides the thinking and behavior of missionaries on a cultural frontier, and
this was certainly true among the friars in New Spain.[143] The
pro-indigenous approach of Franciscan missionaries in New
Spain may be an extension of the philosophy of Franciscan
John Duns Scotus. Several specific dimensions of Bernardino's work reflect this philosophy.

In Bernardino, his pioneering methodologies and overall
ethnographic project, we can perceive Franciscan respect for
the human dignity of all peoples, including the socially mar-
ginalized. He invested his life's effort in meeting, interviewing, and interpreting them and their worldview. He valued
them. While others – in Europe and New Spain – were de-
bating whether or not they were human or had souls, he was
seeking to understand who they were, how they related to
each other, what they believed, and how they found meaning
in the world. The native peoples had dignity and merited respect as human beings, and therefore, their culture merited
understanding. He fell in love with their culture. Even as he

---

[142] Mary Beth Ingham, C.S.J., *Scotus for Dunces: An Introduction to
the Subtle Doctor* (St. Bonaventure, NY: Franciscan Institute Publications,
2003).

[143] Sylvest, *Motifs of Franciscan Mission Theory in Sixteenth Century
New Spain Province of the Holy Gospel.*

expressed disgust with their sacrifices and their "idolatries," he spent five decades investigating Aztec culture with curiosity, creativity, and passion. He pursued his research in community with his students, and gave explicit credit to them as collaborators.

Bernardino is among the greatest Catholic missionaries of this era, and deserves to be recognized along with Dominican Bartolomé de las Casas and Jesuit Mateo Ricci. He used scientific investigations to humanize and improve Franciscan evangelization project. He was a social scientist who researched the Aztecs and their culture in order to express God's love to them. His life is a witness to creating new knowledge to further love.

CHAPTER FIVE
FRANCISCAN SCIENCE TODAY

> We must ask ourselves whether both science and re-
> ligion will contribute to the integration of human cul-
> ture or to its fragmentation. It is a single choice, and
> it confronts us all ... simple neutrality is no longer
> acceptable.
>
> Pope John Paul II[144]

What conclusions can we draw from these three examples? Can we draw lessons from retrieving this tradition
of Franciscan science that are relevant today? These three
Franciscans justify the term "intellectual tradition," for
their work extends beyond philosophy and theology. These
friars linked their intellectual work at universities with the
broader religious and social project of the Franciscans. They
studied at the Universities of Oxford, Paris and Salamanca.
Fortified by their academic training, they travelled to serve
the Order, Church and world in places like Magdeburg and
New Spain. In the context of medieval science, their intellectual work was remarkable, and they contributed to the
learning of many over centuries. They belong in the company
of Bonaventure, Scotus and other Franciscan scholars.

This essay has narrated the stories of three Franciscans
who participated in the science of their respective eras. They
were medieval scientists, but their teaching and research
contributed to the paradigms of their times, and helped medi-

---

[144] Letter of Pope John Paul II To the Reverend George V. Coyne, S.J. Director of the Vatican Observatory. Text in *L'Osservatore Romano* (Weekly edition in English), xxi, n.46 (1064), November 14, 1988.

eval science evolve toward what we now call the natural and social sciences. Although they rarely referenced Francis, they manifest a Franciscan sensibility. With very few exceptions, the scholars who have studied them are not Franciscan, and are thus not trained to perceive the influence of Franciscan training on these three friars.

At least three Franciscan values appear consistently in the vocations and work of these friars. They understood, like Francis, that nature is good because it was created by God, and can lead one to God. Since creation discloses God's creativity, studying nature – using the best available intellectual tools – allows us to learn about God, God's character, and about God's activity in the world. Bartholomew taught his students about creation so they could pray more fruitfully. Roger studied light and the Earth because he believed in so doing he could better understand God. Bernardino perceived God's handiwork in Aztec people and culture, and nature in Mesoamerica. These three friars understood the study of nature to be valuable in and of itself, but also as a practice that could help them acquire wisdom. For them, the study of nature was a religious activity.

Second, they conducted their scientific work in community. They participated – as Franciscan friars – in their respective scholarly communities. Bartholomew's book was written in a Franciscan classroom in dialogue with his students, but was broadly perceived to have value over subsequent generations. Roger learned from the pioneering Oxford Franciscans, taught in Paris, and composed an educational reform program for the Pope. Bernardino helped found a school, taught there, recruited alumni to assist him in his investigations and in paintings, and wrote the *Historia General* as a missionary manual for his fellow friars, and to explain to authorities in Europe what was actually happening in New Spain. Thus, for these Franciscans, the process of scientific inquiry was social, and took place in service to others.

Third, their scientific research had a moral purpose: to improve preaching, and to benefit Church and society. Franciscan science exists to help us live better lives together and with God. In this sense, Franciscan science itself is a form of wisdom. It does not exist for its own sake, but rather to help us grow in love. Bartholomew prepared young friars for ministry in foreign lands. Roger was convinced that reforming education could reform Church and society. Bernardino did not sail to New Spain for the purpose of research, but found that his intellectual skills were needed to improve the Franciscan evangelization project in that place. For these three friars, the pursuit of scientific knowledge was inherently good, but it was always directed toward the goal of fostering love of neighbor and God.

How was the Franciscan tradition of science lost? This is an important question, but a difficult one to answer. The Franciscan tradition of science did not successfully make the transition to the modern scientific paradigm for several reasons. The Catholic Church resisted the challenges to its authority posed by modern science, and became at times defensive. Many modern scientists were hostile to religion, and dismissed faith as superstition. After the scientific revolution, science work became much more expensive and required narrow specialization. The nineteenth century was particularly brutal for religious orders in Europe, with many secular governments persecuting and forcibly suppressing religious life. For example, the Franciscan friars declined in number by eighty percent over a period roughly coinciding with the nineteenth century.[145] In this political context, pursuing science was difficult for many members of religious orders. The broader question of how the Franciscan tradition of science has been lost – or taken from us – merits more study.

How might those of us working within Franciscan institutions and networks approach the retrieval of Franciscan science? There may be parallels in the "rediscovery" of Aristotelian science in the middle ages. A contemporary retrieval of Franciscan science will require an approach distinct from the retrieval of philosophy and theology. It will require a dif-

---

[145] George Marcil, O.F.M., "The Franciscan School through the Centuries," in *The History of Franciscan Theology*, ed. Kenan B. Osborne, OFM (St. Bonaventure, NY: The Franciscan Institute, 1994; reprinted 2007).

ferent retrieval methodology. The retrieval of Franciscan science needs to take contemporary science seriously, but also to take an appropriately skeptical stance toward the ethical implications of science and technology, and toward the religious-like faith in science held by many people today. This essay demonstrates how Franciscans understood the relationship between science and religion as a partnership. This is predicated on the assertion that science and religion are different kinds of knowledge. Both are valid and valuable ways of knowing, powerful in their own way, and each contributes to such a partnership. There are many complex and troubling moral issues that are raised by the rapid expansion and power of science over the past generation, but the process of learning about creation and culture continues to be an inherently good moral act. Retrieving the Franciscan tradition of scientific inquiry would fulfill the constructive engagement of science and religion that Pope John II called for, as quoted at the opening of this chapter.

What might Franciscan science look like today, in the twenty-first century? A contemporary approach to Franciscan science needs to be viewed within the broader framework of knowledge for love. Franciscan science will investigate natural and social phenomena with the same tools as other contemporary forms of study, but integrate this knowledge with love and wisdom, and an awareness of the human dimension of science. Franciscan science always has a moral purpose. Three possibilities present themselves, all of them reflecting Franciscan values in service to the world.

One contemporary analogue to medieval Franciscan science could be found in the rise of ecological literacy. David Orr, a preeminent American philosopher of environmental education, coined the term "ecological literacy," which he defines as the ability to understand and live within the natural systems that make life on Earth possible.[146] He advocates a holistic approach to science and the environment, in which ethics and values are integral to learning. He cri-

---

[146] David Orr, *Ecological Literacy: Education and the Transition to a Postmodern World* (Albany: State University of New York Press, 1992).

tiques American higher education for perpetuating environmental problems by presenting knowledge divorced from a moral framework. He argued that a fundamental purpose of higher education must be to prepare leaders to guide us to a more sustainable human society. There are parallels between what Bartholomew wrote about the religious purpose of understanding creation and what David Orr has said about ecological literacy. His educational vision is coherent with a contemporary Franciscan worldview. We can weave together ecological knowledge with ecological wisdom to create a more integral and faithful approach to Franciscan environmental education.[147]

A second possibility, analogous to Bernardino's groundbreaking anthropological investigations, would be the fostering of greater cultural understanding. The purpose would be to foster mutual respect among human beings and their cultures, and to enhance the practice of solidarity through an awareness of the dignity inherent in all peoples and cultures. Bernardino life and work show that this has been part of the Franciscan intellectual tradition. This could be pursued using social science to enhance mutual understanding of the belief systems, cultural practices, and the understanding of nature within other cultures. Science could play a constructive role in creating a culture of life, as articulated by Pope John Paul II, as well as the kind of globalization in which the Gospel values could be realized, as Pope Benedict XVI has articulated.[148]

A third example would be in the area of public health. Many Franciscan women and men have worked throughout the centuries to provide medical care for poor and un-

---

[147] Keith Douglass Warner, O.F.M., "The Incarnation Matters! Retrieving Franciscan Science for Ecological Literacy," *Association of Franciscan Colleges and Universities Journal* 8, no. 1 (2011). See also Ilia Delio, O.S.F., Keith Douglass Warner, O.F.M., and Pam Wood, *Care for Creation: A Contemporary Franciscan Spirituality of the Earth* (Cincinnati: St. Anthony Messenger Press, 2008).

[148] This would fulfill the vision of Benedict XVI. See Pope Benedict XVI, *Caritas En Veritate* (San Francisco: Ignatius Press, 2009).

derserved communities.[149] Bartholomew described plagues; Roger described the ethical responsibilities of physicians; Bernardino was witness to the devastation of Old World diseases on indigenous New World peoples. Public health takes seriously the poverty and social marginalization of those with health needs, and addresses the broader social systems that give rise to inequity and disease. Natural approaches to healing, following the examples of ethnobotany described by Bernardino, may be quite appropriate for Franciscan science, or perhaps some blend of Western science and naturopathy. This kind of health care, and health care training, would make Francis proud.

Franciscan science today should build upon core Franciscan values: the recognition that God is present in all of creation; the creation of educational processes that further moral and religious conversion; and the engagement with communities in solidarity that are in need of greater justice, peacemaking and care for creation. Do we agree with Bartholomew when he claims "earthly things can lead us to an understanding of heavenly things and to reconciliation with God"? Our Franciscan tradition is not dualistic; it does not split the spirit from the embodied; it leads us into the mystery and truth of the incarnation.

The lives of Bernardino, Bartholomew and Roger are witnesses to a Franciscan integral approach to knowledge. They manifested a holistic approach to the pursuit of knowledge, and understanding that knowledge is for love. Franciscans do not fear scientific knowledge; rather, they are concerned that it be used for the good, to further our own conversion, and deepen our prayerful encounter with God. The example of these three friars reminds us that we have a Franciscan tradition of science that merits retrieval. Franciscan science is a necessary dimension to living out Franciscan spirituality as a wisdom tradition. Knowledge can and must support the pursuit of wisdom, as Bonaventure reminds us. In the Fran-

---

[149] Elise Saggau, O.S.F., ed., *Franciscans and Healthcare: Facing the Future* (St. Bonaventure, NY: Franciscan Institute, 2001); Judith Schaeffer, "Inspired by Franciscans of the Thirteenth Century," *The Cord* 59, no. 1 (2009).

ciscan tradition, science and faith can be authentic partners, as Pope John Paul II insists in the epigraph at the beginning of this chapter. For, as Albert Einstein reminds us, "Science without religion is lame. Religion without science is blind."[150]

---

[150] Albert Einstein, "Religion and Science," *New York Times Magazine* (1930).

FURTHER READING

For an overview of medieval natural history and science, Edward Grant (1996) *The Foundations of Modern Science in the Middle Ages: Their Religious, Institutional, and Intellectual Contexts,* Cambridge, Cambridge University Press, and Grant (2007) *A History of Natural Philosophy: From the Ancient World to the Nineteenth Century,* Cambridge, Cambridge University Press. The best overview of the life and vocation of Bartholomew and his worldbook can be found in Keen, E. (2007) *The Journey of a Book: Bartholomew the Englishman and the Properties of Things,* Canberra, ANU E-press; this can be found on the World Wide Web. A popular account of Roger can be found in Clegg, B. (2003) *The First Scientist: A Life of Roger Bacon,* New York, Carroll & Graff Publishers. This book also has an extensive bibliography. A helpful collection of scholarly studies can be found in Hackett, J. (Ed.) (1997) *Roger Bacon and the Sciences: Commemorative Essays,* Chicago, University of Chicago Press. The best introduction to Bernardino is in León-Portilla, M. (2002) *Bernardino de Sahagún: The First Anthropologist,* Norman, University of Oklahoma Press. To appreciate the beauty of the paintings in *Historia General*, consult the Wikipedia entry and the Wikimedia commons material.

SELECT BIBLIOGRAPHY

Anderson, Arthur J. O. "Sahagún: Career and Character." In *Florentine Codex: Introductions and Indices*, edited by Arthur J. O Anderson and Charles E. Dibble, 29-44. Salt Lake City: University of Utah Press, 1982.

Armstrong, Regis, O.F.M. Cap., J.A. Wayne Hellman, O.F.M. Conv., and William Short, O.F.M., eds. *Francis of Assisi: Early Documents, Volume I: The Saint*. New York: New City Press, 1999.

Bernardino de Sahagún. *Florentine Codex: General History of the Things of New Spain (Translation of and Introduction to Historia General De Las Cosas De La Nueva España; 12 Volumes in 13 Books)*. Translated by Charles E. Dibble and Arthur J. O Anderson. Salt Lake City: University of Utah Press, 1950-1982.

Borgia Steck, Francisco, O.F.M. *El Primer Colegio De America: Santa Cruz De Tlatelolco*. Mexico: Centro de Estudios Franciscanos, 1944.

Carney, Margaret, O.S.F. "The Feminine Side of Franciscan Theology." In *The History of Franciscan Theology*, edited by Kenan B. Osborne, OFM. St. Bonaventure, New York: Franciscan Institute Press, 1994.

Cato, James, ed. *The History of the University of Oxford*. Oxford: Clarendon Press, 1984.

Chenu, Marie-Dominique, O.P. *Nature, Man, and Society in the Twelfth Century: Essays on New Theological Perspectives in the Latin West*. Translated by Jerome

Taylor and Lester K. Little. Chicago: The University of Chicago Press, 1968.

Clegg, Brian. *The First Scientist: A Life of Roger Bacon*. New York: Carroll & Graff Publishers, 2003.

Cousins, Ewert. *Bonaventure: The Soul's Journey into God, the Tree of Life, the Life of St. Francis*, The Classics of Western Spirituality. New York: Paulist Press, 1978.

Delio, Ilia, O.S.F., Keith Douglass Warner, O.F.M., and Pam Wood. *Care for Creation: A Contemporary Franciscan Spirituality of the Earth*. Cincinnati: St. Anthony Messenger Press, 2008.

Edmonson, Munro S., ed. *Sixteenth-Century Mexico: The Work of Sahagún*. Albuquerque, New Mexico: University of New Mexico Press, 1974.

Einstein, Albert. "Religion and Science." *New York Times Magazine* (1930): 1-4, http://www.sacred-texts.com/aor/einstein/einsci.htm, accessed January 2, 2010.

French, Roger, and Andrew Cunningham. *Before Science: The Invention of the Friars' Natural Philosophy*. London: Scolar Press, 1996.

Gates, William. *An Aztec Herbal: The Classic Codex of 1552*. Mineola, New York: Dover Publications, 1939/2000.

Grant, Edward. *The Foundations of Modern Science in the Middle Ages: Their Religious, Institutional, and Intellectual Contexts*. Cambridge: Cambridge University Press, 1996.

————. *A History of Natural Philosophy: From the Ancient World to the Nineteenth Century*. Cambridge: Cambridge University Press, 2007.

Greetham, D.C. "The Concept of Nature in Bartolomaeus Anglicus." *Journal of the History of Ideas* 41, no. 4 (1980): 663-77.

Hackett, Jeremiah. "Roger Bacon and the Sciences: Introduction." In *Roger Bacon and the Sciences:*

Commemorative Essays, edited by Jeremiah Hackett, 1-8. Chicago: University of Chicago Press, 1997.

————. "Roger Bacon: His Life, Career and Works." In *Roger Bacon and the Sciences: Commemorative Essays*, edited by Jeremiah Hackett, 9-26. Leiden: Brill, 1997.

Hackett, Jeremiah. "Roger Bacon on the Classification of the Sciences." In *Roger Bacon and the Sciences*, edited by Jeremiah Hackett, 49-65. Leiden: Brill, 1997.

Hayes, Zachary. "Franciscan Tradition as Wisdom Tradition." *Spirit and Life: A Journal of Contemporary Franciscanism* 7 (1997): 27-40.

Hayes, Zachary, O.F.M. "The Cosmos, a Symbol of the Divine." In *Franciscan Theology of the Environment: An Introductory Reader*, edited by Dawn M. Nothwehr, O.S.F. Quincy, IL: Franciscan Press, 2002.

————. *The Gift of Being: A Theology of Creation*. Collegeville: The Liturgical Press, 2001.

Ingham, Mary Beth, C.S.J. *Scotus for Dunces: An Introduction to the Subtle Doctor*. St. Bonaventure, NY: Franciscan Institute Publications, 2003.

Johnson, Timothy J. "Preaching Precedes Theology: Roger Bacon on the Failure of Mendicant Education." *Franciscan Studies* 68 (2010): 83-97.

Jordan of Giano. "Chronicle of Jordan of Giano." In *Early Franciscan Classics*, edited by David Temple, O.F.M. Oakland: Franciscan Fathers of the St. Barbara Province, 1954.

Keen, Elizabeth. *The Journey of a Book: Bartholomew the Englishman and the Properties of Things*. Canberra: ANU E-press, 2007.

Kuhn, Thomas. *The Structure of Scientific Revolutions*: Chicago: University of Chicago Press, 1962.

Lara, Jaime. *City, Temple, Stage: Eschatological Architecture and Liturgical Theatrics in New Spain*. South Bend: University of Notre Dame, 2005.

León-Portilla, Miguel. "Bernardino De Sahagún: Pioneer of Anthropology." In *Sahagún at 500: Essays on the Quincentenary of the Birth of Fr. Bernardino De Sahagún*, edited by John Frederick Schwaller. Berkeley: Academy of American Franciscan History, 2003.

————. *Bernardino De Sahagún: The First Anthropologist*. Norman: University of Oklahoma Press, 2002.

Lidaka, Juris G. "Bartholomaeus Anglicus in the Thirteenth Century." In *Pre-Modern Encyclopaedic Texts -- Proceedings of the Second Comers Congress, Groningen, 1-4 July 1996*, edited by Peter Binkley, 393-406. Leiden: Brill, 1997.

Lindberg, David C. "Introduction." In *Roger Bacon's Philosophy of Nature: A Critical Edition of De Multiplicatione Specierum and De Speculis Comburentibus*, edited by David C. Lindberg. South Bend: St. Augustines Press, 1998.

————. "Medieval Science and Its Religious Context." *Osiris* 10 (1995): 60-79.

————. "Roger Bacon on Light, Vision, and the Universal Emanation of Force." In *Roger Bacon and the Sciences*, edited by Jeremiah Hackett. Leiden: Brill, 1997.

Little, Andrew G. "The Franciscan School at Oxford in the Thirteenth Century." *Archivum Franciscanum Historicum* 19 (1926): 803-74.

Little, Andrew G. *The Grey Friars in Oxford*. Oxford: Clarendon Press, 1891.

————. *Studies in English Franciscan History*. Longmans, Green & Co.: London, 1916.

López Austin, Alfredo. "The Research Method of Fray Bernardino De Sahagún: The Questionnaires." In

Sixteenth-Century Mexico: The Work of Sahagún, edited by Munro S. Edmonson, 111-50. Albuquerque: University of New Mexico Press, 1974.

————. "Sahagún's Work and the Medicine of the Ancient Nahuas: Possibilities for Study." In *Sixteenth-Century Mexico: The Work of Sahagún*, edited by Munro S. Edmonson, 205-24. Albuquerque: University of New Mexico Press, 1974.

Marcil, George, O.F.M. "The Franciscan School through the Centuries." In *The History of Franciscan Theology*, edited by Kenan B. Osborne, O.F.M., 311-30. St. Bonaventure, N.Y.: The Franciscan Institute, 1994, reprinted 2007.

Mathes, Michael. *The Americas' First Academic Library: Santa Cruz De Tlatelolco*. Sacramento: California State Library, 1985.

McEvoy, James. *Robert Grosseteste*. New York: Oxford University Press, 2000.

Meier, Christel. "Organisation of Knowledge and Encyclopaedic Ordo: Functions and Purposes of a Universal Literary Genre." In *Pre-Modern Encyclopaedic Texts. Proceedings of the Second Comers Congress, Groningen, 1-4 July 1996*, edited by Peter Binkley, 103-26. Leiden: Brill, 1997.

Nicholson, H. B. "Fray Bernardino De Sahagún: A Spanish Missionary in New Spain, 1529-1590." In *Representing Aztec Ritual: Performance, Text, and Image in the Work of Sahagún*, edited by Eloise Quiñones Keber, 21-39. Boulder: University of Colorado Press, 2002.

Okasha, Samir. *Philosophy of Science: A Very Short Introduction*. London: Oxford University Press, 2002.

Orr, David. *Ecological Literacy: Education and the Transition to a Postmodern World*. Albany: State University of New York Press, 1992.

Phelan, John Leddy. *The Millennial Kingdom of the Franciscans in the New World*. Berkeley: University of California Press, 1970.

Pope Benedict XVI. *Caritas En Veritate*: San Francisco: Ignatius Press, 2009.

Power, Amanda. "A Mirror for Every Age: The Reputation of Roger Bacon." *English Historical Review* 121, no. 492 (2006): 657-92.

Ricard, Robert. *The Spiritual Conquest of Mexico*. Berkeley: University of California Press, 1966.

Robertson, D. "The Sixteenth Century Mexican Encyclopedia of Fray Bernardino De Sahagún." *Journal of World History* 4 (1966): 617-27.

Robertson, Donald. *Mexican Manuscript Painting of the Early Colonial Period*. New Haven: Yale University Press, 1959.

Roest, Bert. *A History of Franciscan Education (c. 1210-1517)*. Leiden: Brill, 2000.

Roger Bacon. *Opus Majus*. Translated by Robert Belle Burke. New York: Russell & Russell, 1267/1962.

Röling, Niels. "The Emergence of Knowledge Systems Thinking: A Changing Perception of Relationships among Innovation, Knowledge Process and Configuration." *Knowledge and Policy: The International Journal of Knowledge Transfer* 5, no. 1 (1992): 42-64.

Saggau, Elise, O.S.F., ed. *Franciscans and Healthcare: Facing the Future*. St. Bonaventure, NY: Franciscan Institute, 2001.

Schaeffer, Judith. "Inspired by Franciscans of the Thirteenth Century." *The Cord* 59, no. 1 (2009): 41-53.

Schwaller, John Frederick, ed. *Sahagún at 500: Essays on the Quincentenary of the Birth of Fr. Bernardino De Sahagún*. Berkeley: Academy of American Franciscan History, 2003.

Se Boyar, Gerald E., O.F.M. "Bartolomeus and His Encyclopedia." *The Journal of English and Germanic Philology* XIX (1920): 168-89.

Seymour, M. C. *Bartolomaeus Anglicus and His Encyclopedia*. Aldershot, UK: Variorum, 1992.

Sullivan, Thelma D. *Primeros Memoriales: Paleography of Nahuatl Text and English Translation*. Edited by Arthur J.O. Anderson with H.B. Nicholson, Charles E. Dibble, Eloise Quiñones Keber, and Wayne Ruwet, Vol. 200, Civilization of the American Indian. Norman: University of Oklahoma Press, 1997.

Sylvest, Edwin Edward. *Motifs of Franciscan Mission Theory in Sixteenth Century New Spain Province of the Holy Gospel*. Washington DC: Academy of American Franciscan History, 1975.

Taylor, E.G.R. "Compendium Cosmographiae: A Text-Book of Columbus." *Scottish Geographical Magazine* 47 (1931): 214-19.

Twomey, Michael W. "Appendix: Medieval Encyclopedias." In *Medieval Christian Imagery: A Guide to Interpretation*, edited by R. E. Kaske, Arthur Groos and Michael W. Twomey, 182-215. Toronto: University of Toronto Press, 1988.

Warner, Keith Douglass, OFM. "The Incarnation Matters! Retrieving Franciscan Science for Ecological Literacy." *Association of Franciscan Colleges and Universities Journal* 8, no. 1 (2011): 1-14.

————. "Pilgrims and Strangers: The Evangelical Spirituality of Itinerancy of the Early Franciscan Friars." *Spirit and Life: A Journal of Contemporary Franciscanism* 10 (2000): 63-170.

————. "Teaching Environmental Scientists from Country: Integral Wisdom for a New Australia." *Learning Communities: International Journal of Learning in Social Contexts* 2, no. 1 (2010): 102-14.

Weisheipl, J. A. "Science in the Thirteenth Century." In *The History of the University of Oxford*, edited by James I. Cato, 435-71. Oxford: The Clarendon Press, 1984.

Woodward, David, and Herbert M. Howe. "Roger Bacon on Geography and Cartography." In *Roger Bacon and the Sciences*, edited by Jeremiah Hackett. Leiden: Brill, 1997.